# Contents

# Introduction

*DEALING WITH DEPRESSION* is Volume 334 in the **ISSUES** series. The aim of the series is to offer current, diverse information about important issues in our world, from a UK perspective.

## ABOUT DEALING WITH DEPRESSION

Around one in four people in the UK will experience a mental health issue each year, and a large proportion of these issues is related to depression or anxiety.

This book covers issues that young people may feel that they face with depression, some of the articles offer advice on different types of treatments available and how they can be accessed. Other articles focus on the personal experiences of depression and how they deal with their condition.

## OUR SOURCES

Titles in the **ISSUES** series are designed to function as educational resource books, providing a balanced overview of a specific subject.

The information in our books is comprised of facts, articles and opinions from many different sources, including:

⇨ Newspaper reports and opinion pieces

⇨ Website factsheets

⇨ Magazine and journal articles

⇨ Statistics and surveys

⇨ Government reports

⇨ Literature from special interest groups.

## A NOTE ON CRITICAL EVALUATION

Because the information reprinted here is from a number of different sources, readers should bear in mind the origin of the text and whether the source is likely to have a particular bias when presenting information (or when conducting their research). It is hoped that, as you read about the many aspects of the issues explored in this book, you will critically evaluate the information presented.

It is important that you decide whether you are being presented with facts or opinions. Does the writer give a biased or unbiased report? If an opinion is being expressed, do you agree with the writer? Is there potential bias to the 'facts' or statistics behind an article?

# Useful weblinks

www.blurtitout.org

www.bupa.co.uk

www.cam.ac.uk

www.channel4.com

www.fullfact.org

www.huffingtonpost.co.uk

www.independent.co.uk

www.ncb.org.uk

www.ncmh.info

www.nhs.uk

www.ox.ac.uk

www.princes-trust.org.uk

www.skillsyouneed.com

www.theconversation.com

www.theguardian.com

www.theweek.co.uk

www.youngscot.org

## ASSIGNMENTS

In the back of this book, you will find a selection of assignments designed to help you engage with the articles you have been reading and to explore your own opinions. Some tasks will take longer than others and there is a mixture of design, writing and research-based activities that you can complete alone or in a group.

## FURTHER RESEARCH

At the end of each article we have listed its source and a website that you can visit if you would like to conduct your own research. Please remember to critically evaluate any sources that you consult and consider whether the information you are viewing is accurate and unbiased.

Dealing with Depression

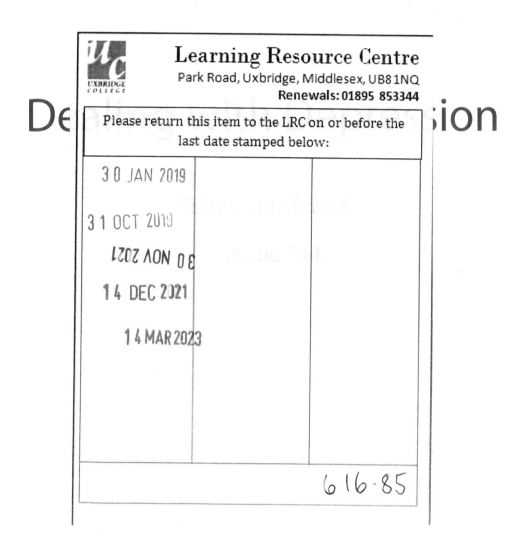

**Independence Educational Publishers**

First published by Independence Educational Publishers

The Studio, High Green

Great Shelford

Cambridge CB22 5EG

England

ISBN-13: 978 1 86168 785 2

## Printed in Great Britain

Zenith Print Group

# Low mood and depression

**D**ifficult events and experiences can leave us in low spirits or cause depression.

It could be relationship problems, bereavement, sleep problems, stress at work, bullying, chronic illness or pain.

Sometimes it's possible to feel down without there being an obvious reason.

## What's the difference between low mood and depression?

A general low mood can include:

⇨ sadness

⇨ feeling anxious or panicky

⇨ worry

⇨ tiredness

⇨ low self-esteem

⇨ frustration

⇨ anger.

But a low mood will tend to lift after a few days or weeks.

Making some small changes in your life, such as resolving a difficult situation, talking about your problems or getting more sleep, can usually improve your mood.

A low mood that doesn't go away can be a sign of depression.

Symptoms of depression can include the following:

⇨ low mood lasting two weeks or more

⇨ not getting any enjoyment out of life

⇨ feeling hopeless

⇨ feeling tired or lacking energy

⇨ not being able to concentrate on everyday things like reading the paper or watching television

⇨ comfort eating or losing your appetite

⇨ sleeping more than usual or being unable to sleep

⇨ having suicidal thoughts or thoughts about harming yourself.

Depression can also come on at specific points in your life, such as the winter months (seasonal affective disorder, or SAD) and after the birth of a child (postnatal depression).

## When to get help for low mood or depression

Whatever the cause, if negative feelings don't go away, are too much for you to cope with, or are stopping you from carrying on with your normal life, you may need to make some changes and get some extra support.

If you're still feeling down after a couple of weeks, talk to your GP or call NHS 111. Your GP can discuss your symptoms with you and make a diagnosis.

## What types of help are available?

If you're diagnosed with depression, your GP will discuss all of the available treatment options with you, including self-help, talking therapies and antidepressants.

### Self-help

Whether you have depression or just find yourself feeling down for a while, it could be worth trying some self-help techniques.

Life changes, such as getting a regular good night's sleep, keeping to a healthy diet, reducing your alcohol intake and getting regular exercise, can help you feel more in control and more able to cope.

Self-help techniques can include activities such as meditation, breathing exercises and learning ways to think about problems differently. Tools such as self-help books and online counselling can be very effective.

If your GP has prescribed antidepressants, it's important that you carry on taking them.

### Talking therapies

There are lots of different types of talking therapies available. To help you decide which one would most suit you, talk to your GP or read about the different types of talking therapies.

In some areas, you can refer yourself directly to your local psychological therapies service.

### Antidepressants

Antidepressants are commonly used to treat depression. There are several types available.

If your GP prescribes you antidepressants, they will discuss the different types and which one would suit you best.

## When to seek help immediately

If you start to feel like your life isn't worth living or you want to harm yourself, get help straight away.

Either see your GP or call NHS 111. You can also call Samaritans on 116 123 for 24-hour confidential, non-judgemental emotional support.

*4 January 2016*

⇨ The above information is reprinted with kind permission from NHS Choices. Please visit www.nhs.uk for further information.

*© NHS Choices*

# Types of depression

***Depression can happen to many different people and for many different reasons.***

Depression is categorised in different ways by different health organisations around the world, and there is often considerable overlap between some of the categories. This means that if you are trying to identify the type of depression you, or somebody you know, may be suffering from then it may not be quite as straightforward as just identifying one type of depression from the list on this page.

Although depression can strike in different ways and for different reasons, the resulting experiences may be similar and there may be more than one cause in the same person.

This article attempts to categorise depression first according to its severity and then according to some particular reasons for it.

## Depression categorised by severity

### Major, severe or clinical depression

Everybody has bad days: days when they feel low, in a bad mood and reluctant to face the world, and days when they feel depressed. However, major depression is more than this, can last for weeks or months, and is a serious but treatable illness.

Major depression is a huge problem internationally, and especially in the Western world.

According to the National Institute of Mental Health (NIMH) in the US, about 7% of the adult population suffer from major depression at any given time.

In the UK, figures show that 25% of people will experience a mental health problem each year and that a significant proportion of these problems are depression and anxiety related.

Typical symptoms of major depression may include:

⇨ Extreme sadness and/or feelings of guilt. Such 'melancholic' feelings are often more severe in the morning.

⇨ The loss of pleasure in normal activities. This can include sufferers becoming 'catatonic', where they withdraw from those around them, cutting off ties with friends and family.

⇨ Difficulty concentrating and making decisions, which can adversely affect work and/or studies.

⇨ Tiredness or fatigue, as well as a loss of energy.

⇨ Sleep problems, including insomnia, an inability to 'turn off', and disturbed sleep patterns.

⇨ Low self-esteem which can sometimes lead to repeated thoughts of self-harm and/or suicide.

Major depression is often triggered by high levels of stress such as problems in the sufferers personal or professional life (loss of partner, loss of a job), illness, or abuse of any type including physical, sexual and substance.

### Dysthymia

Dysthymia or chronic depression causes the sufferer to experience a low mood over a long period of time, possibly many years. Depressed feelings may not be constant over this time and periods of normal mood can last for weeks or even months.

Dysthymia is less severe than major depression although the symptoms are often very similar and can include: sadness, low self-esteem, difficulty in concentrating, fatigue and problems with sleep habits and/or appetite. Generally, sufferers are able to continue to function well enough to hold down a job and social relationships.

Dysthymia can be caused by unresolved problems. 'Bottling up' issues over long periods of time can lead to feelings of general dissatisfaction and depression.

### Atypical depression

Atypical depression is often characterised by a sense of heaviness in the limbs. Sufferers can sometimes experience short bursts of happiness so they may not appear quite as 'distant' or 'cut-off' as major depression sufferers.

Symptoms of atypical depression can include tiredness or fatigue, oversleeping, overeating and weight gain.

Atypical depression is associated with external forces and the behaviours of others. The mood of a sufferer can improve in times of success, or when they receive positive attention and praise. This distinguishes atypical depression from major depression when positive events have little or no effect on the sufferer.

Atypical depression is generally less serious than major depression and people can live with it for many years, or even throughout their entire lives.

## Specific kinds of depression

The list above covers the main types of general depression, however there are numerous forms of more specific depression types – which may occur during certain times in life or while dealing with life circumstances and events.

### Situational depression

Also called adjustment disorder or 'stress response syndrome', situational depression is triggered by a stressful or life-changing event, such as job loss, the death of a loved one, trauma, or the end of a relationship. It is about three times more common than major depression, usually less severe, and may clear up over time without help once the event has ended or the person has adapted to their new conditions.

Situational depression is not the same as post-traumatic stress disorder (PTSD), which usually occurs as a reaction to a life-threatening event and tends to be longer lasting. Adjustment disorders, on the other hand, are short-term and rarely last longer than six months.

## Postnatal postpartum depression (PND)

Around 10–15% of women are estimated to experience postnatal depression.

Postnatal depression usually develops within the first month after childbirth, but can start several months or even up to one year after the birth, and can even start during pregnancy.

Many women worry about getting help for postnatal depression – they feel that their depression is irrational and that they should be delighted with their new baby – and many don't realise that the illness can develop quite a long time after the birth.

As PND is quite common, help is available and treatments are usually very successful. It is important to remember that suffering from postnatal depression in no way reflects a lack of mothering skills or love for the baby.

Postnatal depression (PND) is not to be confused with the 'baby blues' which commonly occurs between the 3rd and the 10th day after the birth and includes being weepy, irritable, anxious and generally feeling low.

Small babies are extremely demanding and the baby blues are very common, and many mothers may experience at least some of the symptoms of PND during this time.

## Seasonal affective disorder (SAD)

This is depression that occurs at the same time every year. It is thought to be mostly biological rather than psychological in origin, although it is mostly treated with psychological treatments and light therapy. SAD can be related to the summer or winter months, each with their own symptoms. Autumn and winter symptoms include hopelessness, anxiety, loss of energy, oversleeping, overeating, and difficulty thinking and concentrating. In the summer, it is somewhat different, with more

the many shades...

...of black

irritable characteristics coming out like anxiety, agitation, trouble sleeping and lack of appetite.

## Psychotic depression

People who develop and suffer from psychotic depression experience delusions (false beliefs) and hallucinations (seeing things that aren't really there).

Sufferers are often aware that their thoughts aren't accurate and can feel very embarrassed and upset by them, which, in turn, makes the condition worse.

Psychotic depression is usually treated in a hospital setting.

## Bipolar disorder

Bipolar can be defined as an emotional disorder characterised by mood swings from depression to mania, often quite rapidly.

Bipolar used to be called manic depression. Bipolar disorder is very serious and can cause risky behaviour, even suicidal tendencies.

According to the NHS, about one person in every 100 in the UK is diagnosed with a bipolar disorder.

There are different types of bipolar disorder, including type 1, type 2, rapid-cycling, and hypomanic bipolar disorders. Cyclothymia is a mild form.

## Premenstrual dysphoric disorder (PMDD)

This is a type of depression that affects women during the second half of their menstrual cycles.

Symptoms often include depression, anxiety and mood swings. Not to be confused with premenstrual syndrome (PMS), which affects up to 85% of women and has milder symptoms, PMDD affects about 5% of women and is much more severe. PMDD most commonly affects women in their late-30s to mid-40s.

The symptoms of PMDD are similar to those in major depression with the most common being irritability, plus breast pain and bloating. Premenstrual dysphoric disorder sufferers have an increased risk of suicidal feelings.

⇨ The above information is reprinted with kind permission from Skills You Need. Please visit www. skillsyouneed.com for further information.

# One in four? How many people suffer from a mental health problem?

⇨ A widely-cited 2007 survey found one in four people in England experienced mental illness at various points in that year. This wasn't the original source of the one in four figure, which goes back to the 1980s.

⇨ The finding is regularly misinterpreted as meaning that one in four of us will suffer from a mental illness in our lifetimes.

⇨ The 2007 study measured different conditions in different time frames so the findings can't tell us how many have suffered from mental illness in any one of these periods.

⇨ A more recent version of the survey found that one in six people suffered from a common mental disorder at various points in 2014.

⇨ Separately, the Health Survey for England found in 2014 that one in four people reported having been diagnosed with at least one mental illness at some point in their lives. A further 18% said they'd experienced an illness but hadn't been diagnosed.

## How common is mental illness?

'One in four' is widely cited in the UK as the number of people who suffer from a mental health problem.

The estimate has been around since the 1980s, although a commonly cited source for the figure is the 2007 Adult Psychiatric Morbidity Survey (APMS). This found that 23% of people in England had at least one psychiatric disorder at some point in that year, and a third of these – 7.2% of people – had more than one.

Because each condition included in the 23% figure has a different time frame it's not meaningful to use the data to say this many are ill in every year, or in any other time period. But the findings do suggest that the number suffering over a lifetime will be more than one in four.

The figures are based on whether survey respondents met criteria that indicated certain illnesses and in some cases on follow-up interviews with medical specialists. The methods used vary by condition.

For example, to screen for Post traumatic stress disorder (PTSD), respondents were asked if they had experienced a traumatic event. If they had, they were asked if they had experienced any of ten symptoms, including jumpiness or difficulty sleeping, twice in the past week. Those who answered yes to six of the ten symptoms screened positive for PTSD.

## Newer figures are available, but don't cover the same thing

A more recent Adult Psychiatric Morbidity Survey (covering 2014) was published last year. It doesn't provide an update on the one in four figure though.

It did report that one in six people in England had a common mental disorder (CMD) in the week before they were interviewed for the study. This, according to the researchers, suggested that around this many could be expected to have a CMD at any one time. These CMDs included things like generalised anxiety disorder, obsessive compulsive disorder and panic disorder.

Since 2000, the proportion of women recorded as having a CMD in England has increased, while in men it has stayed relatively stable.

The study also looked at a number of other conditions including personality disorders, PTSD and drug and alcohol dependency.

These figures are only estimates, as the researchers point out, and the true proportion of people with the conditions could vary from these findings. However the researchers describe the study as the "most reliable profile available of mental health in England".

## Lifetime mental illness: uncertain estimates

Because both the 2007 and 2014 surveys looked at different disorders relating to different time frames, we can't attach a time frame to them as a whole.

But the findings from 2007 do suggest that at least a quarter of people, and probably more, will suffer from one of those illnesses in their lifetime. Although three-quarters of the study group were not found to have had any mental health conditions at any point in 2007, some will have previously been ill or will become ill later in life.

The 2014 Health Survey for England also suggests a higher lifetime figure.

It found that 26% of adults reported having ever been diagnosed with at least one mental illness. And a further 18% reported having experienced a mental illness but not having been diagnosed.

That's based on what diagnoses people report having received, and how they view conditions they've had that weren't diagnosed. There are limitations with this kind of approach because, unlike the APMS, it relies on the perceptions of the people surveyed rather than a systematic attempt at diagnosis by experts.

And, since it's trying to measure illness experienced across the lifetimes of those surveyed, it's only as good as the memories of its participants, and in some cases how they self-diagnose their conditions.

There's some evidence to suggest people can tend to see mental health disorders differently to those designing the surveys. 26% of respondents to a 2013 survey of people in Scotland said they had personally experienced a mental health problem at some point in their life-time.

The proportion rose to 32% when asked if a health professional had ever diagnosed them with one or more of a list of 15 different mental health disorders. That suggests some people may not have been aware of the types of conditions that fall under the umbrella term of 'mental health problems'.

## Other evidence on mental health

Research by David Goldberg and Peter Huxley from 1980 found that one in four people in its sample had suffered some sort of mental disorder in a year.

It didn't look at the same conditions as the APMS (so it didn't include drug or alcohol dependence for example).

More recent data is available on the numbers who are in contact with mental health services.

But this doesn't tell you how many people are suffering from a mental health problem, as clearly not everyone who is mentally ill will receive a diagnosis or treatment. Of all the adults who took part in the 2014 APMS, one in eight reported that they were receiving mental health treatment at the time of the study.

*11 August 2017*

⇨ The above information is reprinted with kind permission from Full Fact. Please visit www.fullfact.org for further information.

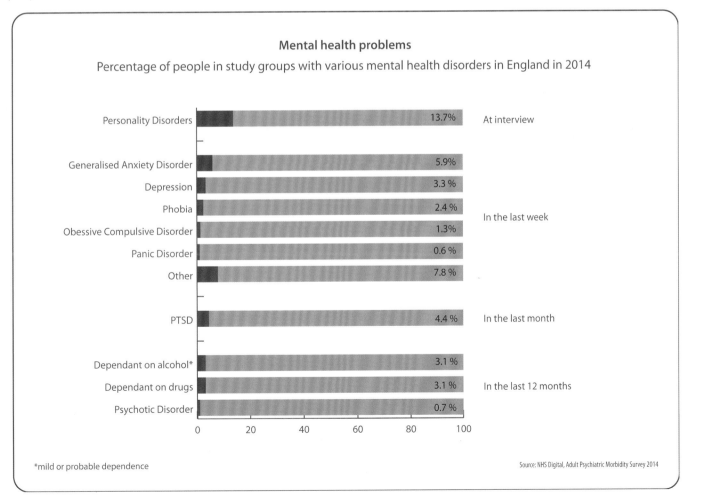

**Mental health problems**
Percentage of people in study groups with various mental health disorders in England in 2014

| Disorder | Percentage | Time frame |
| --- | --- | --- |
| Personality Disorders | 13.7% | At interview |
| Generalised Anxiety Disorder | 5.9% | |
| Depression | 3.3 % | |
| Phobia | 2.4 % | In the last week |
| Obsessive Compulsive Disorder | 1.3% | |
| Panic Disorder | 0.6 % | |
| Other | 7.8 % | |
| PTSD | 4.4 % | In the last month |
| Dependant on alcohol* | 3.1 % | |
| Dependant on drugs | 3.1 % | In the last 12 months |
| Psychotic Disorder | 0.7 % | |

*mild or probable dependence

Source: NHS Digital, Adult Psychiatric Morbidity Survey 2014

# One in five college students have anxiety or depression. Here's why

THE CONVERSATION

**An article from** The Conversation.

*By David Rosenberg, Professor of Psychiatry and Neuroscience, Wayne State University*

Many of us think of college as a wondrous time of new experiences and great freedom to explore new ideas and find one's true self.

In recent years, however, depression and anxiety have afflicted college students at alarming rates. As noted in the latest Centre for Collegiate Mental Health report, anxiety and depression are the top reasons that college students seek counselling.

Research shows that nearly one in five university students are affected with anxiety or depression.

So why are these disorders so prevalent in our college students? As a professor of psychiatry and a practising psychiatrist who has experience with mental health problems among college students, I see a number of factors.

## Dangers in technology

Social media and technology are among the most dangerous of these factors. Excessive use of each tends to engender impaired social interactions and an increased sense of isolation.

Excessive social media use also fosters a certain competition between one's real life and one's virtual life. That is, a tug of war between being engrossed in posting experiences on social media, sending texts and taking selfies instead of enjoying the moment for what it's worth.

Many college students are living dual virtual and real lives, and the virtual life is competing and at times becomes more important than real life. This is not only something that those of us in the trenches see clinically but it has been well-documented in research studies.

Several other studies have found that mobile phone addiction, as well as excess smartphone use, is also associated with increased sleep disturbance, depression, anxiety and overall stress.

For example, one study found that almost 50 per cent of college students indicated they woke up at night to answer text messages. The same study found that the more people use technology during their sleeping hours, the poorer the quality of their sleep and the higher their rates of depression and anxiety.

## Seeking out drugs

But there are other culprits, such as the desire to get into a good college – and stay in college with good grades. To attain these goals, it is not uncommon for students and their parents to seek chemical assistance.

In the past five years, the number of requests I receive from high school and college students and their parents for stimulants such as Ritalin and Adderall has skyrocketed. A decade ago, I rarely, if ever, got such a request. Now, I get several per month. These requests are often made prior to taking major exams, such as finals, the MCAT or the LSAT. For those who are curious, I never acquiesce to these requests and instead recommend a comprehensive psychiatric assessment to make an accurate diagnosis and determine the most appropriate treatment, if one is necessary. The conversation often stops there.

Author David Rosenberg, a psychiatrist, says students are increasingly seeking out drugs meant for people with attention deficit hyperactivity disorder to do better on college exams.

While these medicines can be very effective and safely prescribed in patients with attention deficit hyperactivity disorder, there is considerable risk when they are used for other reasons. It is well-known that side effects from Ritalin and Adderall include anxiety and depression. This risk is even higher in people taking the medicine for an unapproved reason or who do not take the medicine as prescribed.

Another factor at play is that rates of depression in our society have increased significantly over the past 20 years. This means more parents of college students have higher rates of depression. And since depression has a significant genetic component, the risk for depression in the children of a depressed parent is much higher than in the general population.

College students who reported being victims of cyber-bullying in high school – which has nearly doubled in the past decade – also had significantly higher rates of anxiety and depression.

Cigarette smoking has been associated with significantly more sleep problems in college students and increased risk for depression and anxiety. Fortunately, the rate of cigarette smoking and e-cigarette use continues to decline with the rate of past-month use declining to around 16 per cent of college students in 2016.

College students with a history of attention deficit hyperactivity disorder also have much higher rates of anxiety and depression. It is estimated that between two to eight per cent of college students struggle with symptoms of this disorder.

## Other stressors

Moreover, while going to college can be exciting for many, for some the adjustment is hard with profound homesickness and separation anxiety.

These students are at very high risk for depression and anxiety.

Financial stresses brought about by the rising cost of college, including the dread of debt and fear of not getting a job after college and having to move back in with mum and dad after graduation, are associated with increased risk for depression and anxiety in college students.

In the past, it was taken for granted that our children would surpass their parents. Now that is not so. Many college students believe that they will not be able to accomplish as much as their parents did. There is a sense of frustration and that there are no 'good' jobs out there anymore.

Parents are also more involved in their children's college and work experience. It is not uncommon for parents to call college counsellors, bosses and work managers. Once that would have been absolutely off-limits. Now, this is commonplace.

Such parental over-involvement can foster dependence, anxiety and depression, and thwart creativity. I do not mean to blame parents who are concerned and who want the best for their children. However, sometimes failing or not getting an A on a test can be more instructive and instil a

sense of resilience and the ability to 'bounce back'.

So what do we do to curtail anxiety and depression among college students?

## Help, hotlines and hope

Tough problems do not always yield simple, easy solutions. Having an insurance card, 24-hour helplines and hotlines can provide a false sense of security and belief that excellent care is available. However, one study that looked at mental health service use in university students found that even when universal access to mental health care is provided, most students with mental disorders do not get treatment.

The good news is that if we are proactive there is a solution that is cost-effective and that can work, but only if there is buy-in at every level of the particular university and society.

And, ironically, while technology can be a source of anxiety and depression, it can also be used to treat depression. That is, computers, iPads and smartphones can be used to virtually bring a mental health professional to the student where he or she is, be that in their dorm room or off campus.

The key is recognising those at highest risk and who are most vulnerable early. Colleges have to respond on day one and confront the stigma that still follows those with mental illness. Training peer support groups is vital. This is not something to be done in isolation but under the guidance, supervision and training of experienced psychiatrists, psychologists and psychiatric social workers.

Most of all, students and parents need to know from the very beginning of the college experience that the physical and mental well-being of students matters. Colleges should let parents and students know that there are trained and qualified people who can help students at risk discreetly and confidentially.

*9 February 2018*

⇨ The above information is reprinted with kind permission from *The Conversation*. Please visit www.theconversation.com for further information.

# Why stress is more likely to cause depression in men than in women

**An article from The Conversation.**

THE CONVERSATION

*Shervin Assari, Research Investigator of Psychiatry, University of Michigan*

According to the World Health Organization (WHO), more women are affected by depression than men. This pattern is seen in countries around the world, including the United States.

Cross-national and cross-cultural studies have indicated that the prevalence of depression among women is higher at any given time than among men. This pattern does not seem to have many exceptions.

Why is that? Biological differences between men and women, like hormones, explain part of it. These are examples of sex differences. But social factors between men and women (gender differences) may play a bigger role. For instance, women, in general, experience more stress than men, and research has shown that social stress is a main cause of depression.

But, new research that I've conducted with my colleague Maryam Moghani Lankarani suggests that men might be more vulnerable to depression caused by stressful events.

## Why are more women depressed than men?

Researchers have defined stress as any major changes to the status quo (existing balance) that may potentially cause mental or emotional strain or tension. These stressful life events can include marriage, divorce, separation, marital reconciliation, personal injury or illness, dismissal from work or retirement.

Men are more likely to have depressive episodes following work difficulties, divorce and separation. Women, on the other hand, are more sensitive to conflict, serious illness or death happening in their close social network. In fact, research suggests that most of the stressful events that cause depression among women are related to their close social network, such as romantic and marital relationships, child-rearing and parenting.

Research suggests that compared to men, women tend to ruminate (the technical term for 'overthinking') more about stressors and have negative thoughts that cause depression. And at least one study suggests that this explains the gender difference in the prevalence of depression. Rumination can make stress worse, and unfortunately, it is more common among women.

These findings suggest that psychosocial causes of depression may be at least partially gender-specific, and that these disparities are rooted in different life conditions – social inequalities – that men and women experience. And, in general, women tend to experience greater social inequality and social stress, and therefore depression, than men.

The gender gap in depression is largest in countries with highest gender inequalities. Gender difference in burden of depression is highest in the countries where women and men differ more in access to resources and social equity.

And that, oddly, might explain why men might be more susceptible to the depression-inducing effects of stress. They aren't as used to dealing with it.

## Men are more vulnerable to the effects of stress over time

In new research, my colleague Maryam Moghani Lankarani and I found that stressful life events are more likely to predict depression in men than in women.

In fact, men are more susceptible to the depression-inducing effects of each additional stressor over long-term periods.

We looked at data from a nationally representative study that examined how psychological factors affect physical and mental health of individuals over time.

We studied the effects of stressful life events men and women reported at the beginning of the study to their rates of depression 25 years later. We found that the effect of each life stressor on the risk of clinical depression was 50 per cent stronger for men than women.

These findings correspond with a study we published in late 2015 that showed white men may be most vulnerable to the effect of stress on depression, possibly because they have a lower exposure to stress compared to any other demographic group.

It's possible that cumulative exposure to stress may build resilience or habituation to stressors. In other words, people who cope with stress all the time can get used to it.

So the social group exposed to the lowest stressors (living the most privileged life) may at the same time be most vulnerable to each additional stressor. They have not learned to cope with stress as effectively as those who experience it more.

This is potentially the cost of living an easier, and therefore, less stressful life.

## Men who experience depression may not seek care

Men may also be vulnerable to the effects of stress because they may perceive depression as a weakness. They may also define talking about emotion, and seeking help for an emotional problem, such as depression, as a weakness. This is especially the case in developing countries where traditional gender roles are more strongly endorsed.

These beliefs strongly shape behaviours of men who are in need of mental health care, and make men vulnerable when stress and emotional problems happen. All these result in men ignoring depression when it develops, and avoiding care when needed, so as not to look weak.

This also partially explains why more men with depression kill themselves (particularly white men) than women with depression.

Gender influences our risk of depression through various ways. It determines our risk of exposure to adversity. It changes our vulnerability to stress. And it can also determine what resources we'll be able to access to cope with stress or depression.

*22 June 2016*

⇨ The above information is reprinted with kind permission from *The Conversation*. Please visit www.theconversation.com for further information.

# Men affected by depression share what Dwayne 'The Rock' Johnson's comments mean to them

**"Would you tell The Rock to man up?"**

*By Rachel Moss*

Due to his early wrestling career, an acting CV dominated by action roles and his sheer size, Dwayne 'The Rock' Johnson is often heralded as a 'man's man' – an embodiment of everything that is stereo-typically masculine. It is this that makes it all the more poignant that the star has spoken candidly about his experience of depression after his mother's attempted suicide.

"I reached a point where I didn't want to do a thing or go anywhere. I was crying constantly," he told *the Daily Express*, before tweeting his 12.8 million followers to say "depression never discriminates".

"[It] took me a long time to realise it, but the key is to not be afraid to open up. Especially us dudes [who] have a tendency to keep it in. You're not alone," he added.

This isn't the first time Johnson has spoken about his mental ill health, having shared his experiences of depression in his early twenties with CNN in 2015. In light of his recent comments, three men affected by depression share what Johnson's continued efforts to raise awareness of mental ill health mean to them.

Craig Butler, 25, used to find it difficult to speak about depression when he was younger. "A combination of the need to be perceived as 'masculine' and a lack of understanding of the topic made it near impossible to see a benefit to talking about it," he tells HuffPost UK. However, he says seeing Johnson's comments has brought him 'hope'.

"There's still a lot of complexities around the topic if mental health,' he says. "The more people – and men especially – that open up about it, the more normal the issue becomes and thus less dangerous.

"With his persona, I think men like The Rock are crucial in breaking down barriers. For men who don't share the same characteristics, to see someone widely perceived as 'manly' open up will make them feel like they can too... it's something men can aspire to."

Like Butler, Paul Brook, 41, has also found it difficult to be open about his experiences of depression and anxiety in the past. Despite blogging about mental health for almost seven years, he says talking to someone new about his experiences for the first time can still make him feel anxious.

"It's such a personal thing – it's much easier to gloss over it and say 'I'm fine' than to go into what it's really like. I've been lucky that people I've spoken to have been understanding, but depression is so misunderstood that many people will make judgements about you," he tells HuffPost UK. "It seems that every day on Twitter, those who are open about their mental health are subjected to people telling them to 'snap out of it', 'man up', or 'stop feeling sorry' for themselves."

However, he believes when high-profile people like Johnson share their personal experiences it can help to challenge misconceptions.

"I appreciate people being open about their mental health, because I know how hard that can be and what strength it takes to be that honest. When I see someone like The Rock, or Professor Green, or any other man in the public eye, talking openly about what depression feels like, I am full of admiration and respect for them, and glad they've spoken out because people listen to them and pay attention," he says. "Society has expectations about what a man should be like, and these men are brave enough to be honest and defy those expectations."

Gary Parr, 40, has only recently felt comfortable speaking openly about his experiences of depression. "Growing up in Northern Ireland in the 80s wasn't easy, especially where talking about your emotional well-being was concerned," he says. "If you had any problems you were generally just expected to get on with it."

He thinks it's "amazing" a high-profile actor like Johnson has decided to be honest and open about his own problems. "It's inspired me to carry on talking about my own struggles," he says, adding that when men in the public eye talk about mental health "this can only ever be a good thing".

"Such a high-profile star can reach so many people and help break the stigma surrounding mental health. Plus the fact that doing so goes against the stereotypical action man persona he normally portrays should help other men realise there's no shame in suffering from mental health problems," he says.

But as Brook points out, the fact that some people on social media have expressed surprise at Johnson talking about depression shows "how far we still have to go to break the taboos and stigma of mental health".

"It's a normal thing, affecting loads of people – why do we have to be so hush-hush about it?" he asks. "The idea of being 'strong and silent' and not wanting to be seen as 'weak' is poisoning men and putting lives at risk. But would you tell The Rock to 'man up'? He's a big bloke, an action hero, idolised by many, yet he's still suffered with depression. I hope his words make people stop and think."

*3 April 2018*

⇨ The above information is reprinted with kind permission from The Huffington Post UK. Please visit www.huffingtonpost.co.uk for further information.

# One in four girls is depressed at age 14, new study reveals

**Mental ill-health among children of the new century – trends across childhood, with a focus on age 14.**

**New research shows a quarter of girls (24%) and one in ten boys (9%) are depressed at age 14.**

*By Richard Newson*

In this report researchers from the UCL Institute of Education and the University of Liverpool analysed information on more than 10,000 children born in 2000–01 who are taking part in the Millennium Cohort Study.

At ages three, five, seven, 11 and 14, parents reported on their children's mental health. Then, when they reached 14, the children were themselves asked questions about their depressive symptoms.

Based on the 14-year-olds reporting of their emotional problems, 24 per cent of girls and nine per cent of boys suffer from depression.

The research, published with the National Children's Bureau, also investigated links between depressive symptoms and family income. Generally, 14-year-olds from better-off families were less likely to have high levels of depressive symptoms compared to their peers from poorer homes.

Parents' reports of emotional problems were roughly the same for boys and girls throughout childhood, increasing from seven per cent of children at age seven to 12 per cent at age 11. However, by the time they reached early adolescence at age 14, emotional problems became more prevalent in girls, with 18 per cent having symptoms of depression and anxiety, compared to 12 per cent of boys.

Behaviour problems, such as acting out, fighting and being rebellious decreased from infancy to age five, but then increased to age 14. Boys were more likely than girls to have behaviour problems throughout childhood and early adolescence.

As 14-year-olds' own reports of their emotional problems were different to their parents, this research highlights the importance of considering young people's views on their own mental health.

The lead author, Dr Praveetha Patalay, said: "In recent years, there has been a growing policy focus on children's mental health. However, there has been a lack of nationally representative estimates of mental health problems for this generation.

"In other research, we've highlighted the increasing mental health difficulties faced by girls today compared to previous generations and this study further highlights the worryingly high rates of depression."

Professor Emla Fitzsimons, Director of the Millennium Cohort Study, said: "These stark findings provide evidence that mental health problems among girls rise sharply as they enter adolescence; and, while further research using this rich data is needed to understand the causes and consequences of this, this study highlights the extent of mental health problems among young adolescents in the UK today."

Anna Feuchtwang, Chief Executive of the National Children's Bureau, said: "This study of thousands of children gives us the most compelling evidence available about the extent of mental ill-health among children in the UK. With a quarter of 14-year-old girls showing signs of depression, it's now beyond doubt that this problem is reaching crisis point.

"Worryingly, there is evidence that parents may be underestimating their daughters' mental health needs. Conversely, parents may be picking up on symptoms in their sons, which boys don't report themselves. It's vital that both children and their parents can make their voices heard to maximise the chances of early identification and access to specialist support.

"The new research also suggests that signs of depression are generally more common among children from poorer families. We know that mental health doesn't exist in a vacuum and as the Government prepares to publish its plans to improve children's well-being, it must address the overlap with other aspects of disadvantage."

*19 September 2017*

⇨ The above information is reprinted with kind permission from National Children's Bureau. Please visit www.ncb.org.uk for further information.

*© 2018, National Children's Bureau*

# Stigma stopping young people talking about mental health

*Our new research reveals that one in four young people (24%) would not confide in someone if they were experiencing a mental health problem, with many fearing that it could affect their job prospects.*

Our new research reveals that one in four young people (24%) would not confide in someone if they were experiencing a mental health problem, with many fearing that it could affect their job prospects.

The research, funded by Macquarie, based on a survey of 2,215 respondents aged 16 to 25, found that the vast majority of young people (78%) think there is a stigma attached to mental health issues.

A third (32%) of those young people who would keep quiet about their mental health worries think admitting to a problem could affect their job prospects, 57% wouldn't want anyone to know they were struggling and 35% fear it would make them 'look weak'.

Conducted anonymously online, the research found that almost half (47%) of young people have experienced a mental health issue. These young people are:

⇨ Significantly less likely to feel in control of their job prospects[i]

⇨ More likely to feel too tired and stressed to cope with day-to-day life[ii]

⇨ More likely to feel they have no control over their education, training or finances[iii] than their peers.

The findings were published in part two of The Prince's Trust Macquarie *Youth Index*.

Part one was published in January this year and found that the overall well-being of young people in the UK is at its lowest point on the Index since the study was first commissioned in 2009[iv] – with one in four young people not feeling in control of their lives.

In the last year alone, the number of young people supported by The Prince's Trust who are experiencing mental health problems has increased by 16%[v]. In light of these findings, and in a bid to inspire and empower young people, we're calling for people to post on Twitter using the hashtag #TakeControl about the things they do, big or small, that help them to feel in control of their lives[vi].

Dame Martina Milburn DCVO CBE, our Chief Executive, said:

"We know issues like depression and anxiety can have a crippling impact on a young person's aspirations and life chances, so it's alarming to find that so many would rather live with mental health issues than talk to anyone about them.

"We must all work together to instil confidence in these young people that they won't be stigmatised, and one of the key things we can do to help improve their mental health is to help them with their education, training and job prospects.

"Our personal development programmes give young people the self-esteem and coping skills that set them up not just for the workplace but for life."

David Fass, CEO of Macquarie Group, EMEA said:

"It is concerning that one of the reasons young people are reluctant to talk openly about their mental health is that they think it will negatively affect their job prospects. At Macquarie, we encourage our people to bring their whole selves to work and understand that sometimes everyone needs a bit of extra support. Organisations like The Prince's Trust can help young people to develop the skills and

confidence they need to build the future they want; and that's why, as UK employers, we are proud to support this important research."

Professor Louise Arseneault, ESRC Mental Health Leadership Fellow at the Institute of Psychiatry, Psychology & Neuroscience (IoPPN), King's College London said:

"It is extremely worrying to see that young people suffer from the stigma around mental health. This can be a major obstacle for them in seeking help and finding support, which could further affect their confidence in finding work at a crucial stage in their lives. It shouldn't be like this.

"Increasing the understanding and awareness of mental health problems among young people should be a key priority. We also need to explore ways of ensuring young people with mental health problems do not fall out of education or employment from an early age."

As part of our ongoing commitment to help young people overcome any emotional well-being challenges that may be holding them back in life, we've launched a new mental health strategy to give our staff, volunteers and delivery partners the confidence and ability to respond to young people's mental health needs.

We have appointed Chris Harris as our first Mental Health Advisor, a new post funded by Royal Mail Group, and we are forming new partnerships with mental health organisations and specialist services, with the aim of co-locating mental health services at Prince's Trust Centres.

Mental health support will be embedded in all our employability and personal development programmes to help vulnerable young people access the most appropriate care at the earliest opportunity.

[i] 42% of respondents who have experienced a mental health problem don't feel in control of their job prospects, compared to 31% of respondents who have not experienced a mental health problem.

[ii] 47% of respondents who have experienced a mental health problem feel too tired and stressed to cope with day-to-day life, compared to 21% of respondents who have not experienced a mental health problem.

[iii] 24% of respondents who have experienced a mental health problem don't feel in control of their education or training, compared to 12% of respondents who have not experienced a mental health problem. 44% of respondents who have experienced a mental health problem don't feel in control of their finances, compared to 25% of respondents who have not experienced a mental health problem.

[iv] The index, which measures levels of happiness and confidence, has decreased by one point – down from 71 to 70 in the last 12 months.

[v] Financial year 2014–2015. A fifth (21%) of the young people who are supported by The Trust consider themselves to have a mental health problem.

[vI] Posts must be on Facebook, Twitter or Instagram and include the hashtag #TakeControl so that young people can easily find relevant posts.

*1 March 2017*

⇨ The above information is reprinted with kind permission from The Prince's Trust. This information was correct at the time of publishing. Please visit www.princes-trust. org.uk for further information.

*© The Prince's Trust 2018*

## Concerns expressed by all young people compared to those expressed by young people who have experienced a mental health issue

| Concern | All young people | Young people who have experienced a mental health problem |
|---|---|---|
| I don't feel in control of my life | 28% | 39% |
| I feel increasingly out of control of my future | 32% | 41% |
| I don't feel in control of my job prospects | 36% | 42% |
| I didn't believe in myself when I was at school | 45% | 56% |
| I experienced problems during my school/college years that prevented me from focusing on my studies | 48% | 67% |
| Admitting to having a mental health problem could affect my future job prospects* | 32% | 40% |

☐ Young people who have experienced a mental health problem

■ All young people

*These findings represent the views of young people who would not talk to anyone if they thought they were experiencing a mental health problem, not the whole sample

# Cuts to mental health services putting young people at risk, say experts

**Funding cuts and austerity measures are damaging young people's access to mental health services, with potentially long-term consequences for their mental wellbeing, say researchers at the University of Cambridge.**

In an article published today in the *Journal of Public Mental Health*, the team discuss the policy implications of their study published earlier in the year, which found that young people who have contact with mental health services in the community and in clinics are significantly less likely to suffer from clinical depression later in their adolescence than those with equivalent difficulties who do not receive treatment.

Young people's mental health problems are associated with an increased risk of problems later on in adulthood, including poor mental health, lower income, unemployment, inability to maintain a stable cohabiting relationship, and greater contact with the criminal justice system. However, the team's previous study suggested that access for adolescents with mental health problems to intervention in schools and clinics reduces mental health problems up to three years later and would therefore yield personal, economic and societal benefits over an individual's lifespan.

*"We need to acknowledge the mental health suffering in our young people that has only been increasingly apparent in recent years, and resolve to improve young people's access to effective mental health services"*

*Sharon Neufeld*

In the study, Sharon Neufeld and colleagues from the Department of Psychiatry at the University of Cambridge used data obtained between 2005–2010 – prior to funding cuts to Child and Adolescent Mental Health Services in the community and in NHS clinics. Between 2008 and 2013, funding for the services dropped by 5.4 per cent in real terms so that in 2012/2013, only six per cent of the NHS' total mental health budget was spent on these services. The knock-on effect of this was that while in 2005/2006, 38% of 14-year-olds with a mental disorder had made contact with mental health provision for young people in the past year, in 2014/2015 only 25% of all children and young people with a mental disorder had made such service contact.

One consequence of this has been that the number of young people attending A&E due to a psychiatric condition had doubled by 2014/2015, compared with 2010/2011.

"It's important to improve young people's mental health services in schools and strengthen the care pathway to specialist Child and Adolescent Mental Health Services, in order to meet the NHS target of returning contact back up to 35% by 2020/2021," says Mrs Neufeld.

"We need to acknowledge the mental health suffering in our young people that has only been increasingly apparent in recent years, and resolve to improve young people's access to effective mental health services."

She and her colleagues argue that as well as protecting funding for specialist Child and Adolescent Mental Health Services, funding for school-based counselling is also important as their study found that this was the second most used service for young people with a mental health disorder.

"The current Government has promised to provide funding for mental health first-aid training for teachers in secondary schools, which should enable them to better identify those with mental health issues and connect students to the appropriate support services," says Professor Peter Jones. "But this is against a backdrop of freezing school budgets, the very budgets that typically fund school-based counselling.

"Funding for school-based counselling must be ring-fenced, whether it be funded through the education sector or NHS, to ensure young people have adequate service access prior to specialist mental health services."

The researchers also argue that GPs could use more training in identifying mental disorder. The Royal College of General Practitioners reports that nine out of ten people with mental health problems are managed in primary care. However, even in the recent past, most GPs do not include a rotation in mental illness as part of their training. Such gaps in training, say the researchers, mean that GPs correctly identify less than a half (47%) of depression cases.

"This is a huge missed opportunity,' adds Professor Ian Goodyer. 'GPs will encounter a large number of individuals with mental disorders, but have insufficient background knowledge to appropriately identify such cases."

*15 September 2017*

⇨ The above information is reprinted with kind permission from University of Cambridge. Please visit www.cam.ac.uk for further information.

*© University of Cambridge 2018*

# What is postnatal depression?

*Dr Shazia Malik Obstetrician, Gynaecologist, The Portland Hospital, Consultant*

Having a baby is a life-changing experience that brings joy and happiness to parents and their families. However, for some of us, it can take time to feel these positive emotions, as feelings of negativity and depression can be triggered after giving birth.

Postnatal depression is more common than many realise. According to the charity Mind, around 10–15% of new mothers are affected.

Here I explain the differences between 'Baby Blues' and postnatal depression and provide practical tips on what you can do if you think you may have concerns for your own mental well-being or that of someone close to you.

## What are the 'Baby Blues'?

This is a common temporary psychological state soon after childbirth when a new mother may have sudden mood swings; feeling very happy, then very sad, crying for no apparent reason, feeling impatient, unusually irritable, restless, anxious, lonely and sad. It is very common, but only lasts days or a couple of weeks, unlike depression. Although the symptoms are similar, it is not the same as postnatal depression, which is an illness and requires help.

## What is postnatal depression?

This is a form of depression which develops after having a child – typically between six weeks to six months after giving birth. But it can develop at any time, and has all the symptoms of any depressive illness. Whilst there are some risk factors that can predispose a mother to it, the condition can also often strike out of the blue.

### What are the symptoms for postnatal depression?

⇨ Feelings of hopelessness or worthlessness

⇨ Depression

⇨ Anxiety

⇨ Problems bonding with the baby

⇨ Sadness

⇨ Possible feelings of wanting to hurt oneself or the baby

⇨ Insomnia

⇨ Loss of enjoyment of things one normally takes pleasure in

⇨ Difficulty concentrating, or relating to your partner.

In the case of suicidal thoughts or thoughts of harming the baby, postpartum depression is a medical emergency, and medical care should be accessed immediately.

### What should I do if I think I have postnatal depression?

The most important thing is not to ignore your feelings and signs that this is what you might be suffering from. You should talk with your partner, your family, and your GP – especially if you have any thoughts of harming yourself or your baby.

Your health visitor may use a special questionnaire to assess your mental health and well-being if they are concerned, or indeed as a matter of routine.

Your doctor may also do some tests that can check for anaemia or if you have an underactive thyroid gland, which can also cause tiredness, lethargy and feeling under the weather.

It's imperative not to feel that you are unnecessarily troubling anyone – it's so important to seek help as early as possible so that you can get the appropriate help, and enjoy your baby and your life. Also do not fear that your baby will be taken away. Every effort is made to keep you together, even if you need admission to hospital.

### How can postnatal depression be treated?

Treatment depends on each individual's symptoms and circumstances. It can be just psychological support with your GP and self-help groups, through to psychotherapy and medication if required. The medication will depend on if you are breast-feeding or not, so as not to harm your baby. In rare cases some mothers may need admission to hospital for inpatient mental health care.

*19 January 2016*

⇨ The above information is reprinted with kind permission from The Huffington Post UK. Please visit www.huffingtonpost.co.uk for further information.

# Postnatal depression: men get it too

***An article from* The Conversation.**

THE CONVERSATION

*Andrew Mayers, Principal Academic in Psychology, Bournemouth University*

Over the past few years, there has been an increase in media reports about postnatal depression and other maternal mental illnesses, and campaigns have led to greater understanding about the need for more specialist services. Although this is encouraging, very little is said about fathers. But men can get postnatal depression, too.

Currently, only mothers can be diagnosed with postnatal depression. The psychiatrists' 'bible', the Diagnostic and Statistical Manual of Mental Disorders (DSM-5), includes a diagnosis of 'peripartum depression'. Peripartum depression is a form of clinical depression that is present at any time during pregnancy, or within the four weeks after giving birth, although experts working in perinatal mental health tend to be more flexible, extending that period to the first year after giving birth.

In many ways, postnatal depression varies little from traditional depression. It, too, includes a period of at least two weeks where the person experiences low mood or a lack of motivation, or both. Other symptoms include poor sleep, agitation, weight changes, guilt, feelings of worthlessness, and thoughts of death and dying. But the biggest difference is that a depression at this time involves a significant additional person: the child.

Evidence suggests that the long-term consequences of postnatal depression on the child can be damaging, including developmental problems, poor social interaction, partner-relationship problems and greater use of health services (including mental health services).

Around seven to 20% of new mothers experience postnatal depression. A common view is that it is caused by hormonal changes. Although this is partly true, it is far more likely that life factors are responsible, such as poverty, being younger, lack of support and birth trauma. Another potential cause is the sudden overwhelming responsibility of having a baby to care for, and the life changes that it entails.

Depressed mothers also feel intensely guilty about the way they feel about their baby, and fear shame and stigma from society. As a result, at least 50% of mothers will not report a mental health problem. Other mothers will not tell their health provider out of fear of having their child taken away by social services.

## Mounting evidence

All of the above factors can equally apply to fathers. But there is no formal diagnosis of postnatal depression for fathers. Yet evidence from several countries, including Brazil, the US and the UK, suggests that around four to five per cent of fathers experience significant depressive symptoms after their child is born. Some other studies claim that prevalence may be as high as ten per cent.

The cause of these feelings in fathers is similar to what we see with mothers, but there are extra complications. Men are much less likely to seek help for mental health problems, generally.

Societal norms in many nations suggest men should suppress emotion. This is probably even more a factor for fathers, who may perceive their role as being practical and providing for the family. Fathers – especially first-time fathers – might experience many sudden changes, including significant reduction in family income and altered relationships with their wife or partner. These are major risk factors for depression in fathers.

The importance for supporting fathers at this time is as vital as it is for mother. Evidence suggests that a father's depression can have a damaging effect on their child's development. Despite this, it has been shown that fathers are also less likely than mothers to seek help, and that health professionals are less likely to consider that fathers need support, compared with mothers. More evidence is needed to build a case that fathers need support as much as mothers.

## Poorly equipped

It has been argued that, until recently, health professionals have been poorly equipped to recognise and treat mental illnesses associated with the birth of a child. Recent campaigns in the UK have led to changes in policy, funding and health guidelines. However, the recent revision of the National Institute for Health and Care Excellence (NICE) guideline on perinatal mental health does not address fathers' needs. Despite a campaign to address this having support from several professionals and academics, a NICE spokesperson told the BBC that guidelines are unlikely to be changed as there is no evidence that men experience postnatal depression. However, if we discount hormonal factors in new mothers, the remaining risk factors for postnatal depression also apply to fathers. And we need support that recognises that.

*20 November 2017*

# World mental health day: the modern struggle for peace of mind

***The NHS is improving how it treats mental health, but simply isn't equipped to cope with the scale of the crisis in the UK. Is modern life incompatible with mental well-being, asks Richard Carlton-Crabtree?***

Today is World Mental Health Day, and this year is a landmark anniversary. First held in 1992, today is the 25th day dedicated to raising awareness of mental health issues, and to fighting the still-associated stigma.

It is a measure of the progress made over the last quarter century that mental health is now a subject that accrues column inches the whole year round; the prominent Time to Talk and Heads Together campaigns have provided momentum, and even Prince Harry rallied to the cause, which all helps dissipate old prejudices.

In this way, real progress is being made is in the fight to overcome stigma, which sees misplaced attributions of shame that have long been an impediment to those suffering.

Another front in the struggle for mental health is the ongoing effort to ensure that, once people do seek help, they are not let down by a system that fails to provide it – and provide it quickly. In practice, this means rising to the political and logistical challenges of maintaining properly funded and adequately organised mental health services available via the NHS, where progress has been made.

Waiting times remain a problem in many localities, and funding is one aspect of this – but blaming everything on politicians is too simplistic. The evolution of NHS psychological therapy services remains behind their physical health counterparts; they came into being far later, which is why successive governments of all stripes have backed unprecedented levels of investment in the Improving Access to Psychological Therapies (IAPT) Programme, that has trained thousands of new therapists since launching in 2007.

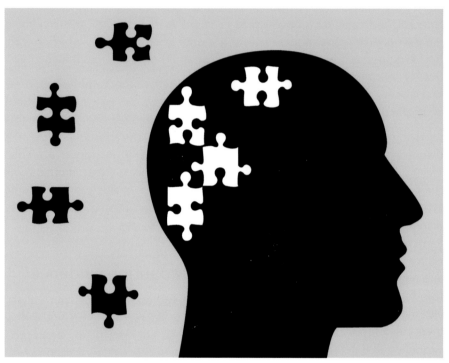

And while governments have a responsibility to properly fund mental health services, the managers and clinicians working in them have a parallel responsibility to make the best use of this funding. In this respect our judgement should not be harsh. Partly as a result of IAPT, our NHS services are fortunate to have some of the most devoted and highly trained therapists in the world, who through their commitment and their skill are making a profound difference to the lives of their service users.

But if we have seen a stepped shift in funding for primary care mental health services, and have some of the world's best people working in them, why has the prevailing narrative on NHS mental health services remained one characterised by complaints about waiting times, accessibility and responsiveness?

The simple fact is, whatever marginal gains are slowly, painfully won 'on the ground' in the struggle for mental health, there is another reality driving waiting times. It is a reality that must be confronted if we are to truly address the issue of mental ill health – and that is the sheer scale of the problem.

The reality of it is that one in four adults will experience a mental illness at some point each year in the UK. Something we never hear is that we only expect to help 15 per cent of them. A decade ago, when the IAPT programme was launched – and heralded as a revolutionary initiative to raise therapeutic capacity on an unprecedented scale – the national target was never to 'meet need' or even to get close to doing so. Instead, it was to increase NHS-commissioned capacity so that it could provide therapy to the 15 per cent of people who could benefit from it – 15 per cent of the one in four prevalence.

Despite being rightly presented as a leap in the right direction, this was also a compromise target, grounded in pragmatic recognition of the low base starting position. On the face of it, an ambition to treat 15 per cent of people in need seems unacceptable. Imagine the outcry if it was openly stated that only 15 per cent of cancer patients, diabetics, or people presenting at A&E with a broken leg would be funded via the NHS.

But here again, context is king; one in four of the UK's adult population is roughly 13 million people. When we pause to consider the issue, it is apparent that we are talking about huge numbers. If all 13 million came forward, our present NHS system would be catastrophically overwhelmed; it is simply not architected to accommodate demand on this scale.

It is in this context that we should consider the unspoken question in the struggle for mental health – why? What is causing mental ill health on such a scale? And what can we do about it?

These are difficult but important questions, and answering them involves confronting another uncomfortable possibility: what if modern life is incompatible with mental well-being for most people? What if the age of technology and globalisation that we are living through is driving a negative sea change in the well-being of our communities? After all, we have seen a financial crisis, falling real incomes, rising levels of temporary employment, the 'middle' squeezed, a housing crisis and a myriad other economic and social upheavals in recent decades.

On top of this, social media has entered our lives, opening us up to more information and opportunities, but also more scrutiny. The gap between the lives that most of us actually lead, and the gilded lifestyles we have access to via the media, Twitter or Instagram, and aspire to, is bigger than ever before. It has even created a modern anxiety – Fear of Missing Out Syndrome (Fomo) and we are increasingly trying to make sure we don't miss out by hooking ourselves to the credit drip.

In past generations, it was just the mortgage that had to be paid monthly; now we have regular payments on credit cards, store cards, cars and even the smartphones that have perpetuated our 'always connected' cycle, and extended the reach of the office beyond the traditional nine to five. Modern life is full, breathless and packed with new pressures. Maybe in the face of these pressures, it is natural that anxiety and depression are on the rise. Modern lifestyles are simply incompatible with positive mental health for some people – for most people, even. We are extending the fringes of human experience and fraying around its edges.

Of course, mental health issues have always existed, even when they weren't recognised as such; bouts of sorrow drowning in gin houses may have been ascribed to fecklessness a century ago, whereas now we might use a modern day equivalent like 'self-medicating', and we must be careful we don't 'over medicalise' a generation of children by teaching them that it's unnatural to be sad occasionally. But the underlying causal dynamics are undoubtedly shifting. Understanding them will be critical if legislators and policy makers are to respond to the problem effectively, because we do have a problem here in the present, and must steel ourselves to deal with it.

But how to do this? How do we get back on the front foot in the struggle for mental health in modern society? This will require us to be clear-eyed about the scale of the issue, and prepare ourselves for a long haul. True prevention may even require a paradigm shift in the balance of our current social and economic structures, and wheels of this size naturally take time to turn. While they are doing so, we must continue the struggle on all fronts – starting with prevention to the fullest extent possible, but also backing our NHS so that it is equipped to meet the challenge wherever it is not.

Although 2017 is the 25th anniversary of World Mental Health Day, it is just

the 10th anniversary of IAPT. In the lifecycle of system change on the scale required, that is the blink of an eye, and dissatisfaction with current NHS services is more a symptom of our stage in the journey, rather than an indication that the direction of travel is wrong.

Plans are now being mobilised to amplify NHS-commissioned primary care therapy, so that it is equal to treating 25 per cent of prevalence by 2020. This is good news, and while this is happening it is appropriate to remember that each of us as individuals also have the power to contribute in this struggle, and do our bit towards building community resilience.

Such is the scale of the issue that it is a rare and fortunate person who is not affected by mental health at some point in their lives, whether themselves or a family member or a friend.

We can help by challenging pejorative attitudes to mental health issues whenever we encounter them, by remembering and including neighbours, friends or relatives who may be lonely or depressed, by easing the burden of each other's many modern pressures with greater consideration, tolerance and understanding in the workplace and the home.

Little day-to-day kindnesses are important; they can have the power to change lives – even to save them. The modern struggle for mental health will be a long and difficult one, but on this day we should take comfort from the knowledge that we are all of us together capable of turning the tide in this struggle, through the simple power of compassion.

*10 October 2017*

⇨ The above information is reprinted with kind permission from *The Independent*. Please visit www.independent.co.uk for further information.

© independent.co.uk 2018

# Ten things that might be making you depressed

*By Julia Pearce*

One in five adults are affected by depression. But why? Are we a generation of inherently sad individuals, or are our lifestyle choices dictating our moods? This article examines ten of the reasons why you might be feeling depressed…

1. **Grief and traumatic experiences:** "Life is a rollercoaster", as Ronan Keating so aptly put it. And with it, life brings various highs and lows, such as relationship difficulties, financial problems or the death of a family member. Some people will be more resilient to the 'lows' than others depending on our personality type. Sometimes it can be difficult to identify a particular event which might have left us feeling depressed, especially if we have buried our feelings for a long time.

2. **Having a lack of purpose:** Research shows that focusing on meaningful goals can buffer the negative effects of stress and other grievances. Without a purpose, our lives can lack a little structure. For example, individuals facing unemployment after years of full-time work often report feeling lost. It is important to remember that we don't have to be saving lives on a daily basis in order to feel a sense of purpose. Focus on the goals which are both meaningful and achievable to you.

3. **Are you getting enough sleep?:** If you're feeling irritable or sluggish on a daily basis, you're not getting enough sleep. John Steinbeck wrote: "A problem difficult at night is resolved in the morning after the committee of sleep has worked on it." He is not entirely wrong. Sleep is a restorative state which allows the body to repair and recharge itself for the day ahead. Experts recommend that adults get between seven and 9 nine hours of sleep a night… and let's face it, we need it!

4.

5. **A poor diet:** Healthy diets are often seen as a yellow brick road to a desired body image, or a prolonged lifespan. But don't forget that your diet can have a huge impact on your mood and subsequently the chances of getting depression. Certain foods promote the maintenance of mood levels.

6. **A lack of exercise:** Research tells us that if you sit still for more than seven hours a day, you increase your likelihood of depression. If you're based in an office, stand up or go for a walk every half an hour. It will not only help boost your mood, but your productivity levels too! Don't neglect your posture, either. Studies have shown that slouching in your chair can make you feel lethargic and put you in a negative mood.

7. **Are you neglecting nature?** If you're feeling depressed, you might be lacking the sunshine hormone, vitamin D. We can get vitamin D from the sun and a number of foods such as red meats and eggs. It is widely recommended that you get at least 15 minutes of natural sunlight a day – but if you're unable to get outside, your doctor might recommend that you take some vitamin D supplements. Going outdoors can be extremely calming and a time to reflect; also known as 'ecotherapy'.

8. **Feelings of isolation or loneliness:** Ask yourself, "how is my social life?" Relationships can help us in times of worry or stress. Allow yourself some time to spend with your friends, family or partner. But remember, it's not about the quantity of friends that you have, it's quality. A toxic relationship with a friend or partner can be a lot more damaging than not having any friends at all. If you've drifted away from family or school friends, force yourself to start a new hobby. It's a great way to meet new people who have something in common with you, and it can be very motivating in the long run.

9. **Stress:** We often don't recognise signs of stress, especially if we have been stressed for a long period of time. But if stress isn't managed effectively, it can not only have drastic effects on our bodies, but on our mental health too. First, identify what makes you stressed. Then, develop some relaxation techniques in order to combat it. We are all different, so try everything until you find out what works for you, and if necessary – see your GP.

10. **Underlying health problems:** Mental and physical health are co-morbid – in other words, one direct affects the other. Some physical illnesses increase our chances of depression; for example: physical disabilities which limit our ability to socialise, exercise or even sleep. Sometimes, other mental health conditions can make us depressed, especially if we don't realise that we have them in the first place.

11. **Self-criticism:** Daniel Radcliffe said: "Being self-critical is good; being self-hating is destructive." Asking yourself, "why did I do that?", or "how could I do this better?" can help us to improve as individuals. However, being self-loathing such as saying, "I'm no good at anything" can be damaging to our mental health. Give yourself a break. Smile at yourself in the mirror or write a list of things you're good at; just be kind to yourself!

⇨ The above information is reprinted with kind permission from The National Centre for Mental Health. Please visit www.ncmh.info for further information.

# Do you have the winter blues?

Lots of people get depressed in winter, or suffer from the 'winter blues'. The medical name for this winter depression is seasonal affective disorder (SAD).

If the short, dark days are getting you down, what can you do to feel like yourself again?

## What causes winter depression?

Despite the fact that millions of us say we've suffered a winter-related low mood, it can feel as though the winter blues is just a myth.

But there's sound scientific evidence to support the idea that the season can affect our moods.

Most scientists believe that the problem is related to the way the body responds to daylight.

Alison Kerry, from the mental health charity Mind, says: "With SAD, one theory is that light entering the eye causes changes in hormone levels in the body.

"In our bodies, light functions to stop the production of the sleep hormone melatonin, making us wake up.

"It's thought that SAD sufferers are affected by shorter daylight hours in the winter. They produce higher melatonin, causing lethargy and symptoms of depression."

If you're going through a bout of winter blues, lack of daylight is probably playing a part.

### Get more light for SAD

If the winter blues is about lack of daylight, it's no surprise that treatment usually involves getting more light into your life.

If you feel low in winter, get outside as often as you can, especially on bright days. Sitting by a window can also help.

You might be tempted to escape the dark winter days with a holiday somewhere sunny.

This can be effective for some, but other SAD sufferers have found that their condition gets worse when they return to the UK.

Light therapy is often used to treat SAD. This involves sitting in front of or beneath a light box that produces a very bright light. Your GP can give you more information.

### Eat yourself happier in winter

It's also important to eat well during the winter. Winter blues can make you crave sugary foods and carbohydrates such as chocolate, pasta and bread, but don't forget to include plenty of fresh fruit and vegetables in your diet.

### Get active to beat SAD

There's another weapon against the seasonal slump: keeping active.

Dr Andrew McCulloch is former chief executive of the Mental Health Foundation, which produced a report on the mental health benefits of exercise.

He says: "There's convincing evidence that 30 minutes of vigorous exercise three times a week is effective against depression, and anecdotal evidence that lighter exercise will have a beneficial effect, too.

"If you have a tendency towards SAD, outdoor exercise will have a double benefit, because you'll gain some daylight."

Activity is believed to change the level of the mood-regulating chemical serotonin in the brain.

It can also help by providing a pleasant change of scene, and helping you meet new people.

If you're suffering from SAD, your GP might be able to refer you to an exercise scheme. But if winter blues is your problem, why not get out and exercise independently?

The charity Mind says research has shown that an hour-long walk in the middle of the day is an effective way to beat the winter blues.

*6 April 2018*

⇨ The above information is reprinted with kind permission from NHS Choices. Please visit www.nhs.uk for further information.

*© NHS Choices 2018*

# Bipolar disorder

***Bipolar disorder, formerly known as manic depression, is a condition that affects your moods, which can swing from one extreme to another.***

People with bipolar disorder have periods or episodes of:

⇨ depression – feeling very low and lethargic

⇨ mania – feeling very high and overactive (less severe mania is known as hypomania)

Symptoms of bipolar disorder depend on which mood you're experiencing. Unlike simple mood swings, each extreme episode of bipolar disorder can last for several weeks (or even longer), and some people may not experience a 'normal' mood very often.

## Depression

You may initially be diagnosed with clinical depression before having a future manic episode (sometimes years later), after which you may be diagnosed with bipolar disorder.

During an episode of depression, you may have overwhelming feelings of worthlessness, which can potentially lead to thoughts of suicide.

If you're feeling suicidal or having severe depressive symptoms, contact your GP, care co-ordinator or local mental health emergency services as soon as possible.

If you want to talk to someone confidentially, call the Samaritans, free of charge, on 116 123. You can talk to them 24 hours a day, seven days a week. Alternatively, visit the Samaritans website or email jo@samaritans.org.

## Mania

During a manic phase of bipolar disorder, you may feel very happy and have lots of energy, ambitious plans and ideas. You may spend large amounts of money on things you can't afford and wouldn't normally want.

Not feeling like eating or sleeping, talking quickly and becoming annoyed easily are also common characteristics of this phase.

You may feel very creative and view the manic phase of bipolar as a positive experience. However, you may also experience symptoms of psychosis, where you see or hear things that aren't there or become convinced of things that aren't true.

## Living with bipolar disorder

The high and low phases of bipolar disorder are often so extreme that they interfere with everyday life.

However, there are several options for treating bipolar disorder that can make a difference. They aim to control the effects of an episode and help someone with bipolar disorder live life as normally as possible.

The following treatment options are available:

⇨ medication to prevent episodes of mania, hypomania (less severe mania) and depression – these are known as mood stabilisers and are taken every day on a long-term basis

⇨ medication to treat the main symptoms of depression and mania when they occur

⇨ learning to recognise the triggers and signs of an episode of depression or mania

⇨ psychological treatment – such as talking therapy, which can help you deal with depression, and provides advice about how to improve your relationships

⇨ lifestyle advice – such as doing regular exercise, planning activities you enjoy that give you a sense of achievement, as well as advice on improving your diet and getting more sleep.

It's thought using a combination of different treatment methods is the best way to control bipolar disorder.

Help and advice for people with a long-term condition or their carers is also available from charities, support groups and associations.

This includes self-help and self-management advice, and learning to deal with the practical aspects of a long-term condition.

## Bipolar disorder and pregnancy

Bipolar disorder, like all other mental health problems, can get worse during pregnancy. However, specialist help is available if you need it.

## What causes bipolar disorder?

The exact cause of bipolar disorder is unknown, although it's believed a number of things can trigger an episode. Extreme stress, overwhelming problems and life-changing events are thought to contribute, as well as genetic and chemical factors.

## Who's affected?

Bipolar disorder is fairly common and one in every 100 adults will be diagnosed with the condition at some point in their life.

Bipolar disorder can occur at any age, although it often develops between the ages of 15 and 19 and rarely develops after 40. Men and women from all backgrounds are equally likely to develop bipolar disorder.

The pattern of mood swings in bipolar disorder varies widely between people. For example, some people only have a couple of bipolar episodes in their lifetime and are stable in between, while others have many episodes.

*26 April 2016*

⇨ The above information is reprinted with kind permission from NHS Choices. Please visit www.nhs.uk for further information.

# What does depression feel like? Trust me – you really don't want to know

*Darker than grief, an implosion of the self, a sheet of ice: no matter how you describe it, this is a terrifying state to be trapped in.*

*By Tim Lott*

This is Depression Awareness Week, so it must be hoped that during this seven-day period more people will become more aware of a condition that a minority experience, and which most others grasp only remotely – confusing it with more familiar feelings, such as unhappiness or misery.

This perception is to some extent shared by the medical community, which can't quite make its mind up whether depression is a physical 'illness', rooted in neurochemistry, or a negative habit of thought that can be addressed by talking or behavioural therapies.

I'm not concerned about which of these two models is the more accurate. I'm still not sure myself. My primary task here is to try to explain something that remains so little understood as an experience – despite the endless books and articles on the subject. Because if the outsider cannot really conceptualise serious depression, the 97.5% who do not suffer from it will be unable to really sympathise, address it or take it seriously.

From the outside it may look like malingering, bad temper and ugly behaviour – and who can empathise with such unattractive traits? Depression is actually much more complex, nuanced and dark than unhappiness – more like an implosion of self. In a serious state of depression, you become a sort of half-living ghost. To give an idea of how distressing this is, I can only say that the trauma of losing my mother when I was 31 – to suicide, sadly – was considerably less than what I had endured during the years prior to her death, when I was suffering from depression myself (I had recovered by the time of her death).

So how is this misleadingly named curse different from recognisable grief? For a start, it can produce symptoms similar to Alzheimer's – forgetfulness, confusion and disorientation. Making even the smallest decisions can be agonising. It can affect not just the mind but also the body – I start to stumble when I walk, or become unable to walk in a straight line. I am more clumsy and accident-prone. In depression you become, in your head, two-dimensional – like a drawing rather than a living, breathing creature. You cannot conjure your actual personality, which you can remember only vaguely, in a theoretical sense. You live in, or close to, a state of perpetual fear, although you are not sure what it is you are afraid of. The writer William Styron called it a 'brainstorm', which is much more accurate than 'unhappiness'.

There is a heavy, leaden feeling in your chest, rather as when someone you love dearly has died; but no one has – except, perhaps, you. You feel acutely alone. It is commonly described as being like viewing the world through a sheet of plate glass; it would be more accurate to say a sheet of thick, semi-opaque ice.

Thus your personality – the normal, accustomed 'you' – has changed. But crucially, although near-apocalyptic from the inside, this transformation is barely perceptible to the observer – except for, perhaps, a certain withdrawnness, or increased anger and irritability. Viewed from the outside – the wall of skin and the windows of eyes – everything remains familiar. Inside, there is a dark storm. Sometimes you may have the overwhelming desire to stand in the street and scream at the top of your voice, for no particular reason (the writer Andrew Solomon described it as "like wanting to vomit but not having a mouth").

Other negative emotions – self-pity, guilt, apathy, pessimism, narcissism – make it a deeply unattractive illness to be around, one that requires unusual levels of understanding and tolerance from family and friends. For all its horrors, it is not naturally evocative of sympathy. Apart from being mistaken for someone who might be a miserable, loveless killjoy, one also has to face the fact that one might be a bit, well, crazy – one of the people who

can't be trusted to be reliable parents, partners, or even employees. So to the list of predictable torments, shame can be added.

There is a paradox here. You want the illness acknowledged but you also want to deny it, because it has a bad reputation. When I am well, which is most of the time, I am (I think) jocular, empathetic, curious, well-adjusted, open and friendly. Many very personable entertainers and 'creatives' likewise suffer depression, although in fact the only group of artists who actually suffer it disproportionately are – you guessed it – writers.

> ### "I have a suspicion that society in its heart of hearts despises depressives because it knows they have a point"

There are positive things about depression, I suppose. It has helped give me a career (without suffering depression I would never have examined my life closely enough to become a writer). And above all, depression, in nearly all cases, sooner or later lifts, and you become 'normal' again. Not that anyone but you will necessarily notice.

But on the whole it's a horror, and it's real, and it deserves sympathy and help. However, in the world we live in, that remains easier to say than do. We don't understand depression partly because it's hard to imagine – but also, perhaps, because we don't want to understand it.

I have a suspicion that society, in its heart of hearts, despises depressives because it knows they have a point: the recognition that life is finite and sad and frightening – as well as those more sanctioned outlooks, joyful and exciting and complex and satisfying. There is a secret feeling most people enjoy that everything, at a fundamental level, is basically OK. Depressives suffer the withdrawal of that feeling, and it is frightening not only to experience but to witness.

Admittedly, severely depressed people can connect only tenuously with reality, but repeated studies have shown that mild to moderate depressives have a more realistic take on life than most 'normal' people, a phenomenon known as 'depressive realism'. As Neel Burton, author of *The Meaning of Madness*, put it, this is "the healthy suspicion that modern life has no meaning and that modern society is absurd and alienating". In a goal-driven, work-oriented culture, this is deeply threatening.

This viewpoint can have a paralysing grip on depressives, sometimes to a psychotic extent – but perhaps it haunts everyone. And therefore the bulk of the unafflicted population may never really understand depression. Not only because they (understandably) lack the imagination, and (unforgivably) fail to trust in the experience of the sufferer – but because, when push comes to shove, they don't want to understand. It's just too… well, depressing.

*19 April 2016*

⇨ The above information is reprinted with kind permission from *The Guardian*. Please visit www.theguardian.com for further information.

# How bad is social media for your mental health?

*In-depth studies link sites such a Facebook with depression but some say they also have benefits.*

The negative effects of social media have been well documented, with Facebook executives even admitting in a recent blog post that the platform may pose a risk to users' emotional well-being.

But while some studies have linked prolonged social media use with symptoms of depression, anxiety and low self-esteem, others suggest it can also provide significant benefits.

Amid all the conflicting research, *The Week* looks at whether the emotional risks of digital technologies outweigh the rewards.

## The negative effects

A number of studies have found an association between social media use and depression, anxiety, sleep problems, eating issues, and increased suicide risk, warn researchers from the University of Melbourne's National Centre of Excellence in Youth Mental Health, in an article on *The Conversation*.

A survey of young people conducted by the London-based Royal Society for Public Health found that social media sites such as Instagram, which primarily focus on people's physical appearance, are "contributing to a generation of young people with body image and body confidence issues".

A study published in the *American Journal of Preventative Medicine* in July examined whether young people's use of 11 social media sites – Twitter, Google+, YouTube, LinkedIn, Instagram, Pinterest, Tumblr, Vine, Snapchat, Facebook and Reddit – correlated with their "perceived social isolation".

"Unsurprisingly, it turned out that the more time people spent on these sites, the more socially isolated they perceived themselves to be. And perceived social isolation is one of the worst things for us, mentally and physically," says Forbes.

A 2015 study by the University of Missouri found that regularly using Facebook could lead to symptoms of depression if the site triggered feelings of envy in the user.

"Facebook can be a fun and healthy activity if users take advantage of the site to stay connected with family and old friends and to share interesting and important aspects of their lives," said Professor Margaret Duffy, who co-authored the report. But if it's used "to see how well an acquaintance is doing financially or how happy an old friend is in his relationship – things that cause envy among users – use of the site can lead to feelings of depression", she adds.

However, care needs to be taken when making a direct link between mental health and social media use, warn the University of Melbourne researchers.

Most studies examining social media and mental health "aren't able to determine whether spending more time on social media leads to depression or anxiety, or if depressed or anxious young people spend more time on social media", they say. "The pathways to mental illness are many and varied, and to suggest mental health problems can be attributed to social media alone would be an oversimplification."

It is also important to note that social media does not affect all people equally, the researchers add, as some individuals may be more susceptible to the negative aspects than others.

## The positive effects

The same University of Missouri study that found a link between Facebook use and depression also found that people who use the platform primarily to connect with others do not experience the negative effects. "In fact, when not triggering feelings of envy, the study shows, Facebook could be a good resource and have positive effects on well-being," *Psychology Today* reports.

There is also compelling evidence that social media can benefit people already dealing with mental health issues by helping them build online communities that provide a source of emotional support. The UK Mental Health Foundation says it is "undeniable" that online technologies can be used to reach the most vulnerable in society, as well as helping to reduce the stigma attached to seeking treatment.

Social media is "invaluable for people with health conditions to know that they are not alone, that there are other people who have gone through this and got better", says Professor John Powell, a public health researcher at Oxford University, who has researched how social media can be used to support people with chronic illnesses.

Matthew Oransky, an assistant professor of adolescent psychiatry at New York's Mount Sinai Hospital, also says many patients make social connections online that they could not find elsewhere, reports *USA Today*. This is particularly true of marginalised teens, such as kids in foster homes and LGBT adolescents, Oransky says.

Research suggests that the manner in which social media is used is key to determining if it is likely to have a positive or negative impact on well-being. For example, active, as opposed to passive, social media use can be beneficial, say the Melbourne researchers. "Although browsing Instagram has been associated with increased depression, talking to others online increases life satisfaction," they say.

## So what is the consensus?

Experts appear to largely agree that social media is neither wholly good nor bad for our emotional well-being, and that its impact on our mental health depends on a number of factors, including how it is used.

And while the risks of these platforms should be acknowledged, so should their potential to help people, especially those already struggling with mental health issues.

*20 December 2017*

⇨ The above information is reprinted with kind permission from *The Week*. Please visit www.theweek.co.uk for further information.

# Ten things people with depression want you to know

### *Young Scot, Dionne McFarlane shared with us her experiences of living with depression.*

For people suffering from depression it can be difficult for people that are close to understand. Depression is the most common mental health issue in the UK. Through my experience of living with depression, this is what I think is important for people to know and try to understand.

## 1. We can't just snap out of it

This can be frustrating to hear, and it shows that the person you're speaking to really doesn't understand how you're feeling. You can't just snap out of depression – it's impossible. I'd describe depression as feeling like drowning – no matter how hard you try to fight back it overpowers you and there's nothing you can do about it. Depression feels like a constant battle and it's exhausting.

## 2. We don't always have a reason as to why we're feeling depressed

This is something I've noticed others find hard to understand. To someone who hasn't ever experienced depression it can be easy to assume that it's caused by an event in someone's life. Depression can be triggered by life events such as bereavement or losing your job, but there doesn't always have to be a reason as to why someone is depressed. Depression can affect anyone and it's an illness. I used to find that before people were understanding about my depression they used to expect there to be a reason as to why I was feeling low and having a bad day when there wasn't a reason and I couldn't explain why I felt the way I was feeling.

## 3. I don't want to hurt you

For friends and family it can be hard to watch someone you love suffer from depression, and it can be difficult to understand how to help and what to do. Depression is a very selfish illness and I find that often we can push people away in order to protect them. With depression there is also feelings of guilt and fear of letting people down. We may take things personally or say something that is horrible but we don't mean it. It can be hard to love and care for someone with depression but standing by someone and showing them unconditional love and care is one of the best things you can ever do for us.

## 4. Depression and being sad are not the same thing

Depression and sadness mean two different things. Sadness is a normal emotion and if something bad was to happen then you may feel sad, but that sadness will lift after a few days. However, depression is a persistent sadness – it can last for weeks, months or even years. It can affect you in various ways such as changing your personality, interests and the way you see the future.

## 5. Depression isn't a choice

We don't choose to be depressed. It can affect various things in your life such as relationships, work and education. We don't choose to have a low mood all the time and find everything an effort. Depression is out of our control, we can't do anything to stop it from happening to us. We aren't weak because we have depression.

## 6. We can feel like a burden and that we're too much to deal with

Depression can cause us to feel like an inconvenience to others, leading us to become feeling isolated and finding it difficult to talk to others. We can sometimes feel that we're too much to deal with and that we're bringing others down. When feeling low we can avoid other people in order to hide how we feel from our family and friends. This is when friends and family need to be compassionate and reassure their loved ones that they're not a burden to them. By letting us know that we can talk to you about how we are feeling, we can gain a sense of safety and support around us.

## 7. Achievements that you see as small are big to me

Achieving goals that we set for ourselves makes us feel proud. Other people's goals may be to get high grades or get a job but sometimes just getting out of bed or talking to someone about how you're feeling is an achievement. Be proud of us when we achieve these goals. These achievements bring us a step closer to recovery and some day we will be able to achieve bigger things, but for now it's about putting one foot in front of the other and achieving little things to give us that sense of accomplishment.

## 8. We can still have some good days

We aren't always having bad days we can still have a good day. We can still have days that are hard but we can also have days when we feel OK and are able to do things. People think that depression is all about having bad days. Truth is, moods fluctuate quite a lot and on good days we can feel like we are in control and that we can achieve something, even just going out with a friend for a coffee. Depression is a mixture of good and bad days. The quote that is one of my favourites is this: "Every day may not be good, but there is something good in every day."

## 9. We appreciate your kind words and how you're trying to help

It can be hard to know what to say and what to do to help. Sometimes offering some kind words can be helpful and we may not seem like we appreciate it but we really do. It can be hard for us to show feelings of gratefulness but the kindness shown really does mean a lot to us.

## 10. We're trying our best to get through it

Depression is something that we have to work through. I've learned that recovery isn't something you choose once – you have to choose it over and over again. We can't just let go and ignore depression, it has to be treated appropriately by a medical professional. If we have to use therapy and/or medication as a way of working through our depression please do stand by us. There's no shame in asking for help. Depression can make us feel isolated and lonely and having someone by our side can make us feel less alone.

⇨ The above information is reprinted with kind permission from Young Scot. Please visit www.youngscot.org for further information.

*© 2018 Young Scot*

# 17 celebrities open up about mental health: Selena Gomez, Demi Lovato, Stormzy and more

*By Natasha Hinde*

**W**hen it comes to mental health, the more people that speak about their experiences, the better.

Unfortunately stigma is still a huge issue in society, affecting nine in ten people with mental health problems. However, as with all things in society, attitudes have the ability change.

Here, we highlight 17 famous people who are helping to slowly chip away at stigma by publicly speaking about mental health.

## Demi Lovato, 24

Demi Lovato spoke about her bipolar disorder diagnosis as part of a campaign for mental health group Be Vocal.

"Getting a diagnosis was kind of a relief," she said. 2It helped me start to make sense of the harmful things I was doing to cope with what I was experiencing. Now I had no choice but to move forward and learn how to live with it, so I worked with my health care professional and tried different treatment plans until I found what works for me.

"Living well with bipolar disorder is possible, but it takes patience, it takes work and it is an ongoing process. The reality is that you're not a car that goes into a shop and gets fixed right away. Everyone's process and treatment plan may be different.

"I am so grateful for my life today and I want to protect it. It isn't always easy to take positive steps each day, but I know I have to in order to stay healthy. If you are struggling today with a mental health condition, you may not be able to see it as clearly right away but please don't give up – things can get better.

"You are worthy of more and there are people who can help. Asking for help is a sign of strength.2

## Professor Green, 33

Chatting to Freddie Flintoff for Heads Together's latest campaign #ItsOkToSay, Professor Green said: "I think I was born with anxiety. I used to take a lot of time off school. I was brought up by my grandmother, my dad was 18 when I was born, my mum was only 16. And my mum was the first person to leave when I was a year old.

"I was 24 and my dad took his own life. And it wasn't until years later when I did a documentary for the BBC and I had a conversation with my nan – it's weird that this happened for the first time on camera – but we spoke about it properly and I broke down.

"And I was petrified, it scared me that people were going to see me at my most vulnerable in a way that I don't often see myself. But that conversation changed everything because from that point, everything was out in the open and I was able to then talk to my friends about it."

## Ellie Goulding, 30

Ellie Goulding has previously spoken about her battle with anxiety and panic attacks, revealing that she underwent cognitive behavioural therapy (CBT) to help her deal with her struggles.

She told *Flare* magazine: "I was sceptical at first because I'd never had therapy, but not being able to leave the house was so debilitating. And this was when my career was really taking off.

"My surroundings would trigger a panic attack, so I couldn't go to the studio unless I was lying down in the car with a pillow over my face. I used to beat myself up about it.

"There were a couple of times after I released 'Delirium' when I was doing promo and thought, 'Oh god, it's coming back, it's coming back,' but it didn't. I think my body has become quite good at controlling anxiety."

## Stormzy, 23

Grime and hip hop artist Stormzy has taken a new approach to discussing mental health, by rapping about his experiences of depression in the single 'Lay Me Bare'.

Speaking to Channel 4 about the track, he said: "If there's anyone out there going through it, I think for them to see that I went through it, it would help.

"Because for a long time I used to think that soldiers don't go through that. You know? Like, strong people in life, the bravest, the most courageous people, they don't go through that, they just get on with it.

"That's not the case. I feel like I always come across confidently and happy. I just present myself in a positive way so I can spread that. So people will be looking at me and thinking I don't go through nothing, so for me to let people know that I do, I felt it's important for me to let people know that."

## Dame Kelly Holmes, 47

Dame Holmes opened up about her depression battle, self-harming and the need to seek help in an open letter which the athlete tweeted during Mental Health Awareness Week.

She wrote: "I suffered in silence. And for too long. Behind closed doors – literally – I self-harmed to try and relieve the depression I was suffering as I struggled to overcome injuries that I thought would end my career.

My body was constantly letting me down and then my mind did as well.

"Looking back, I wonder why I kept my feelings secret for so long. Even after I came through the worst, I didn't let on to people outside of my immediate family.

"Truth is, the stigma attached to mental health 12 years ago was a massive barrier for me. So I kept quiet, held it in and hid my mental health problems.

"Fast forward to today and people are talking more openly about mental health issues. But there's still a long way to go before people talk about mental health as openly as they do about heart disease or cancer."

### Ryan Reynolds, 40

The actor opened up about suffering with lifelong anxiety and the effects the mental illness had on him while filming *Deadpool*.

He told *Variety* "Our father was tough. He wasn't easy on anyone. And he wasn't easy on himself. I think the anxiety might have started there, trying to find ways to control others by trying to control myself. At the time, I never recognised that. I was just a twitchy kid.

"[When filming *Deadpool*] I never, ever slept. Or I was sleeping at a perfect right angle – just sitting straight, constantly working at the same time. By the time we were in post [production], we'd been to Comic-Con, and people went crazy for it. The expectations were eating me alive.

"Blake helped me through that. I'm lucky to have her around just to keep me sane."

### Lena Dunham, 30

Dunham sat down with comedian Jacqueline Novak, on behalf of *Refinery 29*, to discuss her struggles with anxiety.

"I've always been anxious, but I haven't been the kind of anxious that makes you run ten miles a day and make a lot of calls on your Blackberry," she said. "I'm the kind of anxious that makes

you like, 'I'm not going to be able to come out tonight, tomorrow night or maybe for the next 67 nights'."

### Zayn Malik, 24

Malik opened up about having an eating disorder and struggling with anxiety issues.

He told *Sunday Times Magazine*: "Every area of my life was so regimented and controlled it was the one area where I could say, 'No, I'm not eating that". Once I got over the control, the eating just came back into place, super naturally.

"I came back to the UK and spent some time with my mum and got some TLC, and she cooked me food and I got back in touch, mentally, with a lot of the things I'd lost."

Discussing his anxiety struggles, he added: "I now have no problem with anxiety. It was something I was dealing with in the band."

### Lady Gaga, 31

In an open letter to fans about her battle with PTSD, Gaga wrote: "I have wrestled for some time about when, how and if I should reveal my diagnosis of Post Traumatic Stress Disorder (PTSD). After five years of searching for the answers to my chronic pain and the change I have felt in my brain, I am finally well enough to tell you.

"There is a lot of shame attached to mental illness, but it's important that you know that there is hope and a chance for recovery."

### Stephen Fry, 59

In a BBC documentary *The Secret Life of a Manic Depressive*, the comedian, actor and author spoke about being diagnosed with bipolar disorder.

"I'd never heard the word before, but for the first time, at the age of 37, I had a diagnosis that explained the massive highs and miserable lows I've lived with all my life," he said.

"The psychiatrist... recommended I take a long break. I came here to America and for months I saw a therapist and walked up and down this

beach. My mind was full of questions. Am I now mad? How have I got this illness, could it have been prevented, can I be cured of it? Since then, I have discovered just how serious it is to have bipolarity, or manic depression as it's also called. Four million others in the UK have it and many of them end up killing themselves.

"I want to speak out, to fight the public stigma and to give a clearer picture of a mental illness most people know little about."

### Selena Gomez, 24

Gomez has been incredibly open about her poor mental health and how it affects her work and life.

In a previous interview with *Vogue*, she said: "Tours are a really lonely place for me. My self-esteem was shot. I was depressed, anxious. I started to have panic attacks right before getting on stage, or right after leaving the stage. Basically I felt I wasn't good enough, wasn't capable."

In 2016, she said she was taking time off to deal with panic attacks, anxiety and depression which were a side effect of her lupus diagnosis.

She said in a statement: "As many of you know, around a year ago I revealed that I have lupus, an illness that can affect people in different ways.

"I've discovered that anxiety, panic attacks and depression can be side effects of lupus, which can present their own challenges.

"I want to be proactive and focus on maintaining my health and happiness and have decided that the best way forward is to take some time off."

### Prince William, 34

The Duke of Cambridge called for an end to the 'stiff upper lip' culture in a bid to encourage more people to open up about mental health issues - especially men.

He told charity magazine *CALMzine*: "We will all go through tough times in our lives, but men especially feel the need to pretend that everything is OK, and that admitting this to their friends will make them appear weak.

I can assure you this is actually a sign of strength."

### Carol Vorderman, 56

Carol Vorderman has bravely spoken about the debilitating depression she has experienced while going through the menopause and how it led to suicidal thoughts.

She told ITV's *Lorraine*: "This depression hit me – and I don't use the word depression lightly. This was a blackness where I would wake up – nothing else in my life was going wrong, I'm a very lucky woman, no money worries or nothing like that – and I would wake up and think 'I don't see the point in carrying on. I just don't see the point in life.'

"And there was no reason to feel that way and the only reason I didn't do anything, and I've not admitted it before, is because I had two children."

She said that from the moment she started taking medication for it, she felt better.

"I've been fed up, and obviously at the moment my mum is not well so I'm upset," she explained. "But there is a reason for all of those things whereas before there was no reason for it and it was absolutely, categorically to do with hormones."

### Kid Cudi, 33

Last year, the singer shared a candid Facebook post explaining that he'd checked himself into rehab because he was experiencing depression and suicidal thoughts.

"It's been difficult for me to find the words to what I'm about to share with you because I feel ashamed. Ashamed to be a leader and hero to so many while admitting I've been living a lie,' he wrote.

"It took me a while to get to this place of commitment, but it is something I have to do for myself, my family, my best friend/daughter and all of you, my fans.

"Yesterday I checked myself into rehab for depression and suicidal urges. I am not at peace. I haven't been since you've known me. If I didn't come here, I would've done something to myself. I simply am a damaged human swimming in a pool of emotions everyday of my life.

"There's a raging violent storm inside of my heart at all times. Idk (I don't know) what peace feels like. Idk how to relax. My anxiety and depression have ruled my life for as long as I can remember and I never leave the house because of it.

"I can't make new friends because of it. I don't trust anyone because of it and I'm tired of being held back in my life. I deserve to have peace. I deserve to be happy and smiling."

### Cara Delevingne, 24

When rumours were circulating that Delevingne was going to quit modelling, she tweeted: "I suffer from depression and was a model during a particularly rough patch of self hatred.

"I am so lucky for the work I get to do, but I used to work to try and escape and just ended up completely exhausting myself.

"I am focusing on filming and trying to learn how to not pick apart my every flaw. I am really good at that."

### Prince Harry, 32

Prince Harry sat down with Bryony Gordon to discuss how losing his mum – and not grieving properly – affected his mental health.

"I can safely say that losing my mum at the age of 12, and therefore shutting down all of my emotions for the last 20 years, has had a quite serious effect on not only my personal life but my work as well," he explained.

"I have probably been very close to a complete breakdown on numerous occasions when all sorts of grief and sort of lies and misconceptions and everything are coming to you from every angle.

"My way of dealing with it was sticking my head in the sand, refusing to ever

think about my mum, because why would that help? [I thought] it's only going to make you sad, it's not going to bring her back. So from an emotional side, I was like 'right, don't ever let your emotions be part of anything'.

"I was a typical 20, 25, 28-year-old running around going 'life is great', or 'life is fine'. And then [I] started to have a few conversations and actually all of a sudden, all of this grief that I have never processed started to come to the forefront and I was like, there is actually a lot of stuff here that I need to deal with."

### Frankie Bridge, 28

The former Saturdays singer spoke to *Glamour* about her depression battle: "One night, I got upset because Wayne hadn't bought the right yoghurts; I managed to convince myself that he didn't know me at all.

"It set off this spiral of negative thinking – that if I disappeared, it wouldn't matter to anyone. In fact, it would make everybody's life easier. I felt that I was worthless, that I was ugly, that I didn't deserve anything."

She sought help and has since been on the road to recovery.

"Nine times out of ten, my depression is under control," she added. "I get a bit emotional to think I felt so low about myself, that I shouldn't be around people I love, because I can't make them happy. I did lose myself, but I feel like me again now."

*12 May 2017*

⇨ The above information is reprinted with kind permission from The Huffington Post UK. Please visit www.huffingtonpost.co.uk for further information.

# Antidepressants

*Explains what antidepressants are, how they work, possible side effects and information about withdrawal.*

## What are antidepressants?

Antidepressants are psychiatric drugs which are available on prescription and are licensed to treat depression. Some are also licensed to treat other conditions, such as:

⇨ anxiety

⇨ phobias

⇨ bulimia (an eating disorder)

⇨ some physical conditions.

## How do they work?

Antidepressants work by boosting or prolonging the activity of particular brain chemicals, such as noradrenaline and serotonin, which are thought to be involved with regulating mood.

Noradrenaline and serotonin are neurotransmitters. This means that they pass messages between nerve cells in your brain, and between nerves and other target organs in the rest of your body.

By causing a change to your brain chemistry, antidepressants may lift your mood. However, antidepressants don't work for everyone, and there is no scientific evidence that depression is caused by a chemical imbalance which is corrected by antidepressants.

## What different types of antidepressant are there?

There are several different types of antidepressants, which were developed at different times. They all tend to act on the same brain chemicals and cause similar effects, but the different types have different chemical structures, and may have different side effects.

The different types are:

⇨ selective serotonin reuptake inhibitors (SSRIs)

⇨ serotonin and noradrenaline reuptake inhibitors (SNRIs)

⇨ tricyclics and tricyclic-related drugs

⇨ monoamine oxidase inhibitors (MAOIs)

⇨ other antidepressants.

### Selective serotonin reuptake inhibitors (SSRIs)

About SSRIs:

⇨ They were first developed in the late 1980s, so they have been in use for about 30 years.

⇨ They work by blocking the reuptake of serotonin into the nerve cell that released it, which prolongs its action in the brain.

⇨ The side effects that SSRIs can cause are generally easier to cope with than those of other types of antidepressants.

⇨ They're the most commonly prescribed type of antidepressant in the UK.

### Serotonin and noradrenaline reuptake inhibitors (SNRIs)

About SNRIs:

⇨ The first of these was developed in the early 1990s, so they're one of the newer types of antidepressant.

⇨ They're very similar in action to SSRIs, but they act on noradrenaline as well as serotonin.

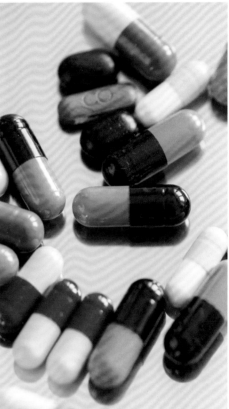

⇨ They have a more selective action than tricyclics, which means they're better at targeting the brain chemicals which affect your mood, without causing unwanted side effects.

⇨ They're sometimes preferred for treating more severe depression and anxiety.

### Tricyclic and tricyclic-related drugs

About tricyclics:

⇨ They're the oldest type of antidepressant, first developed in the 1950s.

⇨ They work by prolonging the action of noradrenaline and serotonin in the brain.

- ⇨ They're called 'tricyclic' because of their chemical structure, which has three rings.

- ⇨ They tend to cause more unpleasant side effects compared with other types of antidepressants.

About tricyclic-related drugs:

- ⇨ They act in a very similar way to tricyclics, but they have a slightly different chemical structure.

- ⇨ They tend to cause more unpleasant side effects compared with other types of antidepressants, but they're less likely to cause antimuscarinic effects than tricyclics.

## Monoamine oxidase inhibitors (MAOIs)

About MAOIs:

- ⇨ They work by making it harder for an enzyme (monoamine oxidase) that breaks down noradrenaline and serotonin to do its job, causing these chemicals to stay active in the body for longer.

- ⇨ They can have dangerous interactions with some kinds of food, so when taking MAOIs, you need to follow a careful diet.

- ⇨ Because of these interactions, you're not likely to be prescribed an MAOI unless you've tried all other types of antidepressant and none of them have worked for you.

- ⇨ They should only be prescribed by specialists.

*2016*

- ⇨ The above information is reprinted with kind permission from *Channel 4 news*. Please visit www.channel4.com for further information.

# Antidepressants more effective in treating depression than placebo

*A major study comparing 21 commonly used antidepressants concludes that all are more effective than placebo for the short-term treatment of acute depression in adults, with effectiveness ranging from small to moderate for different drugs.*

The international study, published in *The Lancet*, is a network meta-analysis of 522 double-blind, randomised controlled trials comprising a total of 11,6477 participants. The study includes the largest amount of unpublished data to date, and all the data from the study have been made freely available online.

An estimated 350 million have depression worldwide. The economic burden in the USA alone has been estimated to be more than US$210 billion. Pharmacological and non-pharmacological treatments are available but because of inadequate resources, antidepressants are used more frequently than psychological interventions. However, there is considerable debate about their effectiveness.

As part of the study, the authors identified all double-blind, randomised controlled trials (RCTs) comparing antidepressants with placebo, or with another antidepressants (head-to-head trials) for the acute treatment (over eight weeks) of major depression in adults aged 18 years or more. The authors then contacted pharmaceutical companies, original study authors, and regulatory agencies to supplement incomplete reports of the original papers, or provide data for unpublished studies.

The primary outcomes were efficacy (number of patients who responded to treatment, i.e. who had a reduction in depressive symptoms of 50% or more on a validated rating scale over eight weeks) and acceptability (proportion of patients who withdrew from the study for any reason by week eight).

Overall, 522 double-blind RCTs done between 1979 and 2016 comparing 21 commonly used antidepressants or placebo were included in the meta-analysis, the largest ever in psychiatry. A total of 87,052 participants had been randomly assigned to receive a drug, and 29,425 to receive placebo. The majority of patients had moderate-to-severe depression.

All 21 antidepressants were more effective than placebo, and only one drug (clomipramine) less acceptable than placebo.

Some antidepressants were more effective than others, with agomelatine, amitriptyline, escitalopram, mirtazapine, paroxetine, venlafaxine and vortioxetine proving most effective, and fluoxetine, fluvoxamine, reboxetine and trazodone being the least effective. The majority of the most effective antidepressants are now off-patent and available in generic form.

Antidepressants also differed in terms of acceptability, with agomelatine, citalopram, escitalopram, fluoxetine,

409 (78%) of 522 trials were funded by pharmaceutical companies, and the authors retrieved unpublished information for 274 (52%) of the trials included in the meta-analysis. Overall, 46 (9%) trials were rated as high risk of bias, 380 (78%) as moderate, and 96 (18%) as low. The design of the network meta-analysis and inclusion of unpublished data is intended to reduce the impact of individual study bias as much as possible. Although this study included a significant amount of unpublished data, a certain amount could still not be retrieved.

The authors note that they did not have access to individual-level data so were only able to analyse group differences. For instance, they could not look at the effectiveness or acceptability of antidepressants in relation to age, sex, severity of symptoms, duration of illness or other individual-level characteristics.

sertraline and vortioxetine proving most tolerable, and amitriptyline, clomipramine, duloxetine, fluvoxamine, reboxetine, trazodone and venlafaxine being the least tolerable.

The authors note that the data included in the meta-analysis covers eight weeks of treatment, so may not necessarily apply to longer term antidepressant use. The differences in efficacy and acceptability between different antidepressants were smaller when data from placebo-controlled trials were also considered.

In order to ensure that the trials included in the meta-analysis were comparable, the authors excluded studies with patients who also had bipolar depression, symptoms of psychosis or treatment resistant depression, meaning that the findings may not apply to these patients.

"Our study brings together the best available evidence to inform and guide doctors and patients in their treatment decisions," said Dr Andrea Cipriani of Oxford University's Department of Psychiatry. "We found that the most commonly used antidepressants are more effective than placebo, with some more effective than others. Our findings are relevant for adults experiencing a first or second episode of depression – the typical population seen in general practice.

"Antidepressants can be an effective tool to treat major depression, but this does not necessarily mean that antidepressants should always be the first line of treatment. Medication should always be considered alongside other options, such as psychological therapies, where these are available. Patients should be aware of the potential benefits from antidepressants and always speak to the doctors about the most suitable treatment for them individually."

The findings from this study contrast with a similar analysis in children and adolescents, which concluded that fluoxetine was probably the only antidepressant that might reduce depressive symptoms. The authors note that the difference may be because depression in young people is the result of different mechanisms or causes, and note that because of the smaller number of studies in young people there is great uncertainty around the risks and benefits of using any antidepressants for the treatment of depression in children and adolescents.

*22 February 2018*

⇨ The above information is reprinted with kind permission from University of Oxford. Please visit www.ox.ac.uk for further information.

# Of course antidepressants work. They've saved my life several times

## *I have had a complicated relationship with these white, pink, turquoise and bright red pills but I remain a staunch advocate of the medication.*

*Kate Leaver*

A major study has just proven that antidepressant medication works. Researchers analysed data from 522 trials involving 115,477 people and declared that the 21 most common antidepressants tested were effective at reducing the symptoms of depression. Given that doctors wrote 64.7 million prescriptions for these vital little pills in 2016 alone, this is something millions of Brits already know.

Depression is affecting great swathes of our population, rendering them morose, exhausted, broken and chemically bereft. I am one of them. I have been taking antidepressants, on and off, for around 17 years. I live with bipolar disorder and I've trialled a staggering number of different antidepressant medications, responding to changes in my body and brain and trying to tweak my treatment plan.

I have had a complicated relationship with these white, pink, turquoise and bright red pills: I've had severe side effects and suffered intense withdrawal symptoms between drugs. Yet I remain a staunch supporter of the antidepressant; a lifelong advocate for SSRIs (selective serotonin reuptake inhibitors) and MAOIs (monoamine oxidase inhibitors). Antidepressants are not perfect, and it is worth noting that they are effective in roughly two-thirds of cases, but they are often all we have to allow depressed people the privilege of living their own lives.

If you are one of the millions of people also taking a pill each morning or evening, then you probably know that these powerful little spheres can save a life, or at the very least make it worth living. If you are not one of those – or worse, you are someone who actively shames people who have to take medication for a valid and debilitating condition – then please, listen. Antidepressants can enable a person to participate in their own life, when they simply cannot otherwise. They have made me able to feel things like joy and love and enthusiasm; they have made me able to function, get out of bed, leave the house, speak to other human beings, work. Without them, these 'trivial' gestures of a normal life can seem gargantuan, even impossible. With the right chemicals in my system, I can live my life. What's more, they keep me from wanting to end it.

With this new study and the confirmation that antidepressants are effective, it is time to start treating them as precisely what they are: medicine. Antidepressant medication is treatment for a health condition that affects a huge number of people. We have spent too long in a society that attaches moral weight to these vital pills; shaming the people who use them and belittling the almighty need for them. There are too many depressed people shying away from treatment because they are frightened or ashamed of taking medication, which is absurd and often tragic. It is medicine, and medicine should not come with stigma.

The research suggests that there are a million more people who would benefit from being on antidepressant medication. This just proves, again, how astonishingly pervasive the illness is. You've heard the stat before: one in four people will experience a mental health problem in their lifetime. One in six report dealing with a common mental illness like depression or anxiety every week. It is almost guaranteed that you know and probably love someone who is affected.

It is crucially important that we stop wasting time judging people for treating a dangerous illness, and start putting our energies towards getting them the services they need to stay alive. It's time to demand better resources from our government, who have a duty of care to the vulnerable and a moral responsibility to improve our mental healthcare services. Following recently announced cuts to funding, current resources are already dangerously insufficient.

So, please, let's listen to the science and absorb the fact that antidepressant medication is effective and necessary for millions of people. Let's continue our work to make it better, change our attitude and increase our compassion to those who need it. And let's stop squabbling over the moral significance of taking a pill to treat your mood – and get people the treatment they need.

*22 February 2018*

⇨ The above information is reprinted with kind permission from *The Independent*. Please visit www.independent.co.uk for further information.

# New ways to treat depression in teenagers

*An article from* **The Conversation.**

*Ian Michael Goodyer, University of Cambridge*

THE CONVERSATION

Around one in 20 teenagers suffers from depression. Episodes can last for several months. Unfortunately, about 50% of teenagers who have a depressive episode are at risk of falling ill again, increasing the likelihood of relationship difficulties, educational failure and poor employment prospects. It's important that treatments have a lasting effect to reduce the risk of becoming ill a second time.

My research investigates the causes of and treatments for adolescent mental illnesses, with a particular focus on depression. One of our key projects is evaluating the importance of various psychological treatments that are effective in helping young people with depression.

Only one treatment – cognitive behavioural therapy (CBT) – is approved by the UK's National Institute for Health and Care Excellence (NICE) for treating depression in teenagers. Unfortunately, there is a shortage of CBT therapists in the UK. This means that many young people with depression are placed on a waiting list, increasing their risk of worsening mental health.

With a growing rate of self-harm among depressed teenagers and no signs of the suicide rate going down, we have arguably reached a tipping point in services where we need to improve availability of therapies using existing mental health staff. With limited resources available for youth mental health in most countries, we need new therapeutic approaches that could be taught more easily than CBT but carry at least the same effectiveness for the depressed teenager.

Our *Improving mood with psycho-analytic and cognitive therapies* (IMPACT) study published in *The Lancet Psychiatry* considered three treatments: cognitive behavioural therapy (CBT), short-term psychoanalytic psychotherapy (STPP) and brief psycho-social intervention (BPI).

CBT in this trial was a 20-session treatment focused on correcting negative thinking about the self, the world and the future, together with efforts to alleviate low mood arising from negative thoughts. STPP is a 28-session psychoanalytic treatment that aims to improve the ability to regulate mood and make and maintain positive relationships. BPI, in contrast, is a 12-session intervention that aims to provide information and explanations about depression, advising on immediate problems including keeping safe at this time of vulnerability, together with caring and support in making decisions about family school and friends.

There is good evidence that CBT works in adolescents. There is evidence that STPP is as good as CBT in adults, but, at the start of the trial we did not know if it worked for adolescents. We used BPI as a reference treatment, likely to be less effective than CBT or STPP because it uses fewer sessions and there is no evidence for or against its effectiveness.

We carried out a randomised controlled trial of 465 teenagers, referred to 15 NHS clinics across England. Each participant had a diagnosis of depression. We wanted to know if STPP is as effective as CBT. We also expected that both of these more intensive and specialist therapies would be more effective than BPI.

Our main goal was to find out which of these therapies showed the most enduring effects a year after the end of treatment. If we could show such a long-term effect we may have revealed a therapy that is not only a useful treatment but, importantly, also reduces the chances of a second episode occurring – something which is very common in teenage years.

## More to choose from

We found that two-thirds of the depressed teenagers from each of the three treatments (CBT, STPP, BPI) showed improvements. Participants who responded continued to do so up to a year after their treatment ended.

Treatment effects (defined as a drop in depression symptoms of 50% or more, 12 months after the end of treatment)

were obtained with between six to 11 sessions of therapy delivered over a three to six-month period for each category. These improvements were had using about half of the sessions planned for each treatment. We believe that many teenagers do not remain in longer-term treatments once they are confident they are functioning reasonably normally again or because they believe there is little likelihood therapy will do them any good.

We are currently analysing detailed information from the patients to understand their experience of treatment and confirm our speculations about the preference for shorter than planned therapy.

The total costs of treatment, including the subsequent use of health and social services after the end of treatment, were no different across the three therapies. The results are important as there is a limited choice of talking therapies. The fact that all three therapies are equally effective, and cost about the same to implement, means that we can now offer alternatives to depressed young people.

The next step is to see how we can target these treatments more precisely to patients' needs as we suspect that there are important individual differences in determining which psychological treatment suits each type of depressed young person. We believe that each of these psychological treatments may have advantages for distinct groups of adolescent depression. Targeting the treatments in a more personalised manner may deliver more efficient and effective therapy and further reduce time to remission as well as lower the risk of further episodes.

*6 March 2017*

⇨ The above information is reprinted with kind permission from *The Conversation*. Please visit www. theconversation.com for further information.

# Cognitive behavioural therapy (CBT)

***Cognitive behavioural therapy (CBT) is a talking therapy that can help you manage your problems by changing the way you think and behave.***

It's most commonly used to treat anxiety and depression, but can be useful for other mental and physical health problems.

## How CBT works

CBT is based on the concept that your thoughts, feelings, physical sensations and actions are interconnected, and that negative thoughts and feelings can trap you in a vicious cycle.

CBT aims to help you deal with overwhelming problems in a more positive way by breaking them down into smaller parts. You're shown how to change these negative patterns to improve the way you feel.

Unlike some other talking treatments, CBT deals with your current problems, rather than focusing on issues from your past. It looks for practical ways to improve your state of mind on a daily basis.

## Uses for CBT

CBT has been shown to be an effective way of treating a number of different mental health conditions.

In addition to depression or anxiety disorders, CBT can also help people with:

⇨ obsessive compulsive disorder (OCD)

⇨ panic disorder

- ⇨ post-traumatic stress disorder (PTSD)
- ⇨ phobias
- ⇨ eating disorders – such as anorexia and bulimia
- ⇨ sleep problems – such as insomnia
- ⇨ problems related to alcohol misuse.

CBT is also sometimes used to treat people with long-term health conditions, such as:

- ⇨ irritable bowel syndrome (IBS)
- ⇨ chronic fatigue syndrome (CFS).

Although CBT can't cure the physical symptoms of these conditions, it can help people cope better with their symptoms.

## What happens during CBT sessions

If CBT is recommended, you'll usually have a session with a therapist once a week or once every two weeks. The course of treatment usually lasts for between five and 20 sessions, with each session lasting 30–60 minutes.

During the sessions, you'll work with your therapist to break down your problems into their separate parts – such as your thoughts, physical feelings and actions.

You and your therapist will analyse these areas to work out if they're unrealistic or unhelpful and to determine the effect they have on each other and on you. Your therapist will then be able to help you work out how to change unhelpful thoughts and behaviours.

After working out what you can change, your therapist will ask you to practise these changes in your daily life and you'll discuss how you got on during the next session.

The eventual aim of therapy is to teach you to apply the skills you've learnt during treatment to your daily life.

This should help you manage your problems and stop them having a negative impact on your life – even after your course of treatment finishes.

## Pros and cons of CBT

Cognitive behavioural therapy (CBT) can be as effective as medication in treating some mental health problems, but it may not be successful or suitable for everyone.

Some of the advantages of CBT include:

- ⇨ it may be helpful in cases where medication alone hasn't worked
- ⇨ it can be completed in a relatively short period of time compared to other talking therapies
- ⇨ the highly structured nature of CBT means it can be provided in different formats, including in groups, self-help books and computer programs
- ⇨ it teaches you useful and practical strategies that can be used in everyday life – even after the treatment has finished.

Some of the disadvantages of CBT to consider include:

- ⇨ you need to commit yourself to the process to get the most from it – a therapist can help and advise you, but they need your co-operation
- ⇨ attending regular CBT sessions and carrying out any extra work between sessions can take up a lot of your time
- ⇨ it may not be suitable for people with more complex mental health needs or learning difficulties – as it requires structured sessions
- ⇨ it involves confronting your emotions and anxieties – you may experience initial periods where you're anxious or emotionally uncomfortable

- ⇨ it focuses on the individual's capacity to change themselves (their thoughts, feelings and behaviours) – which doesn't address any wider problems in systems or families that often have a significant impact on an individual's health and well-being.

Some critics also argue that because CBT only addresses current problems and focuses on specific issues, it doesn't address the possible underlying causes of mental health conditions, such as an unhappy childhood.

## Finding a CBT therapist

If you think you have a problem that may benefit from treatment with CBT, the first step is usually to speak to your GP.

Your GP may be able to refer you for CBT that's free on the NHS, although you may have to wait.

If you can afford it, you can choose to pay for your therapy privately. The cost of private therapy sessions varies, but it's usually £40–100 per session.

If you're considering having CBT privately, ask your GP if they can suggest a local therapist.

The British Association for Behavioural & Cognitive Psychotherapies (BABCP) keeps a register of all accredited therapists in the UK and The British Psychological Society (BPS) has a directory of chartered psychologists, some of whom specialise in CBT.

*15 July 2016*

- ⇨ The above information is reprinted with kind permission from NHS Choices. Please visit www.nhs.uk for further information.

*© NHS Choices 2018*

# Have you felt depressed? Here's how mindfulness might help you

*By Dr Meera Joshi, Mindfulness expert for Bupa UK*

There has been a huge increase in the amount of scientific research into mindfulness-based practices. This is because they can help people struggling with a range of mental health issues, including work-related stress and anxiety. This article focuses on mindfulness and depression.

In short, mindfulness is about paying attention to the present moment. This can help you develop awareness of the things around you, and in turn your thoughts, emotions and bodily sensations.

## Can mindfulness help treat depression?

The National Institute for Health and Care Excellence (NICE) is an organisation that recommends therapies based on the best scientific evidence available. NICE recommends mindfulness for the treatment of recurrent depression. Specifically, they recommend an approach called mindfulness-based cognitive therapy (MBCT).

### What does this mean for me?

An average episode of depression usually lasts between six and eight months. If after a period of feeling better, you relapse and your symptoms come back, this is known as recurrent depression. Mindfulness-based cognitive therapy (MBCT) is a type of mindfulness practice that is used alongside other treatments to help people who've had three or more relapses of depression. The idea is that mindfulness helps you acknowledge, step back from, and watch the whirlwind of thoughts and emotions that can contribute to your low mood. As you practise the skill of mindfulness you can learn to let these thoughts pass rather than getting caught up in them.

### Is there any evidence?

But what's the evidence when it comes to mindfulness and depression? A large study, often referred to as the PREVENT trial, showed that MBCT is as effective as antidepressant medication in preventing further relapses in recurrent depression. In other words, if you are taking antidepressants to prevent another episode of depression, practising MBCT could be just as effective.

### What does treatment with MBCT involve?

MBCT courses are provided by the NHS, so your GP may refer you if they think it's appropriate. A course lasts for eight weeks, with a two-hour session per week led by a trained MBCT practitioner. There could be anything between eight and 15 people in the group. A typical session will involve practical mindfulness exercises and opportunities for you to reflect on your experiences. MBCT sessions will also help you understand how your mind works when you're feeling low. After each session you'll be given some exercises to practise at home.

### I'm depressed; can mindfulness help me with my depression now?

Some studies suggest that mindfulness (MBCT) may well help to treat people who currently have depression. However, this requires further research and approval from NICE. At the moment, NICE specifically recommend MBCT if you have had depression in the past and are at risk of developing it again.

## What do I do next?

If you think that you, or someone you know may be suffering from depression, it's important to get help. If you feel that any of the above may apply to you, please do contact your GP. They'll be able to help and see if MBCT might be suitable for you.

*19 December 2017*

⇨ The above information is reprinted with kind permission from Bupa Please visit www.bupa.co.uk for further information.

# Mindfulness is not a waste of time – it can help treat depression

THE CONVERSATION

*An article from* **The Conversation.**

*Sarah McDonald, Clinical Psychologist and Research Fellow, University of Nottingham*

Mindfulness is about paying attention to the present moment in a non-judgemental way. The practitioner learns to avoid dwelling on the past or worrying about the future. This can be difficult, especially for people suffering from anxiety and depression, but, if achieved, it can bring lasting relief.

NHS mental health services are increasingly offering a therapy called mindfulness-based cognitive therapy (MBCT) which is, as the name suggests, based on mindfulness skills. MBCT is an evidence-based group therapy. It combines training in mindfulness skills and practices with cognitive therapy (learning about managing and changing one's negative thought patterns). MBCT seems particularly effective in reducing the risk of relapse for people who have had three or more episodes of depression.

Research on MBCT is improving in quality and scale, and we are starting to learn how mindfulness practices and therapy work in alleviating depression symptoms. Despite this, some people remain sceptical of mindfulness in general and MBCT in particular.

## Answering the critics

Those who see mindfulness as having been corrupted into a therapy from its Buddhist roots may take issue with mindfulness, as might those who incorrectly think it is just meditation.

To the first argument, I would suggest that when ideas cross boundaries, it's likely that everyone benefits. Surely Buddhists are pleased that their practices are being used to relieve suffering. However, it is important that clinicians ensure that mindfulness is practised as intended (which links to the second point about mindfulness not just being meditation), and it helps that people who understand the origins of mindfulness continue to scrutinise therapeutic approaches labelled as 'mindfulness-based'.

There is a difference between MBCT, a tailored and researched package of therapy based on psychological theory, and 'mindfulness therapies', which could cover almost anything.

Other critics (correctly) point to research studies that show no significant benefit of MBCT over antidepressant drugs. The presence of studies showing similar outcomes for people receiving MBCT and people taking antidepressants could be seen as a reason not to favour MBCT. However, for some people, developing skills to enable them to ward off depression might seem preferable to taking medication for long periods.

There are now robust studies showing beneficial effects for MBCT in preventing depressive relapse, particularly for those who have had multiple relapses in the past, and those who have experienced childhood trauma.

## Getting to the deeper meaning

What about the mechanisms behind MBCT? How does mindfulness training reduce depression? First, as we would expect, MBCT is meant to increase people's mindfulness skills – non-judgemental acceptance, being able to see thoughts as just thoughts rather than as commands that have to be acted on – and people who rate themselves as having higher levels of mindfulness skills at the end of therapy are at less risk of relapsing than those taking antidepressants. Having these skills helps people notice their own tendencies to fall into negative thinking cycles, and then to be able to stand back rather react emotionally to them.

Beyond this, there are indirect mechanisms of MBCT affecting depression. 'Indirect' means that MBCT changes a way of thinking or feeling, and this change then reduces the risk of depressive relapse.

Indirect mechanisms may include reducing emotional reactivity (how quickly negative thoughts and feelings are triggered by current events), repetitive negative thoughts, de-centring (the ability to consider multiple aspects of a situation) and rumination. These mechanisms are being investigated in increasingly rigorous studies and the early signs suggest that a deeper understanding of how and why MBCT works to alleviate major depression may not be far away.

*27 May 2016*

⇨ The above information is reprinted with kind permission from *The Conversation*. Please visit www.theconversation.com for further information.

# Depression: habits that help us through

Depression is rough. When we're in the thick of it, life can feel incredibly difficult. Even the simplest tasks can feel overwhelming, and the things we used to enjoy become meaningless.

While we can't magically make depression go away (if only we could!), there are healthy habits we can adopt that might help ease the pain a little and reduce the severity of our symptoms.

## Depression habits that help us through

At Blurt we like to think of these positive actions as our 'Mental Health Toolkit'. When utilised regularly, they can bring more joy to our good days, and help us through our difficult ones.

## Habits that help

We are all unique. Just as our experiences of depression vary, so too will the habits that help us. Broadly speaking though, they fall with four main areas, which we will look at in turn.

### 1. Looking after our bodies

Our mind and body don't work in isolation of each other. Research into the mind-body link has found many connections between our mental and physical health.

It follows then, that taking steps to look after our bodies can help our mental well-being. Granted, it can feel incredibly difficult when we're unwell, but paying attention to things like our diet, exercise and sleep can have a positive effect on our mental health – even though we might not feel the benefits straight away.

### Ideas to try

Here are some things members of our community keep in their Mental Health Toolkit to help look after their bodies:

⇨ *Massage. Chiropractic. Meds. Relaxing Baths. Walks outside.*

⇨ *I keep easy to prepare food in the house or freezer to make sure I eat proper meals when I don't feel up to cooking or shopping. Store cupboard basics are good too. Pesto, beans, rice, pasta.*

⇨ *Exercise classes help me loads, I do Zumba, Clubbercise, spin, pump and Pilates and they always give me the escape I need.*

Other things we might want to try could include: making time to relax, taking steps to improve our sleep, taking nutrition supplements, limiting our consumption of stimulants (alcohol, caffeine, sugar, etc.), exploring complementary and alternative therapies.

### 2. Building relationships

Depression can be horribly isolating. When we're struggling, seeing other people can feel like the last thing we want to do. However, making connections with others – feeling heard, seen and understood – is central to our well-being. Our relationships (if healthy) can provide us with much-needed support, comfort and solace.

### Ideas to try

Here's how relationships help members of our community:

⇨ *Asking for help: I find if I am honest and tell people how I'm struggling, they do rally round and that helps even if it makes me feel guilty!*

⇨ *I have also found that getting a dog has helped with my mental health because I have a new purpose in life and I feel safe/calm with her always by my side.*

⇨ *Other things we might want to consider could include: seeking professional support (our GP, counsellors, etc.), reaching out to people, building healthy personal boundaries, volunteering.*

### 3. Cultivating a positive mindset

Yes, we know: the term 'positive mindset' can feel grating (if not downright offensive) when we're battling the blackness of depression. We don't CHOOSE to feel low, and getting better isn't simply a case of pulling our chin up and plastering on a smile.

However, working on our mindset – doing things like challenging our negative thoughts, being self-compassionate, and practising mindfulness – can change how we feel about ourselves in the long term.

## Ideas to try

Here are a few things our community members find helpful:

⇨ *Making myself be really 'present' in the moment, focussing on what's around me and what I'm doing rather than thinking back or ahead.*

⇨ *Taking myself out into the garden feeling the wind/air on my face like a caress, seeing the plants surviving against all odds… really helps me a lot*

⇨ *Speaking to myself kindly, resting when I need to.*

Other things we might want to try could include: challenging self-critical thoughts, practising gratitude, appreciating beauty, working on self-esteem and imposter syndrome, meditating, saying no (or yes!) more, setting goals.

## 4. Practising self-care

At Blurt we are ALWAYS harping on about self-care – and with good reason. It really can be life changing. Taking time to do the things we enjoy, that nourish, comfort and inspire us, that get us in that wonderful state of 'flow' can make profound changes to our well-being.

Self-care doesn't need to be fluffy or expensive – there's a whole range of things we can do.

## Ideas to try

Here are just a few of the things our community have in their self-care arsenal:

⇨ *My MH toolkit includes snuggling up on the sofa with a fluffy blanket a Film or Netflix with a cup of Rooiboos tea and my crochet – for ultimate comfort and relaxation.*

⇨ *A nice bath and face pack*

⇨ *Reading a book*

⇨ *Walk in the sunshine*

⇨ *Listening to music*

⇨ *Cuddles with my son*

⇨ *Colouring in books with neon gel pens and crafty kits to make stuff.*

⇨ *I have a self-soothe box of things that work for me. Inside I have photos of me with my friends, photos of our old cats, pictures of my fave dog breeds, soft toy hedgehog, tangle toy, stress ball, lavender oil, collection of nice stones, paper to rip up, elastic bands, sudoku book, soft hair scrunchies, friendship bracelets, temporary motivational tattoos, those metal puzzle things you get in crackers, e.g. separate the ring from the coil by twisting, dark chocolate, cute cards I've been given, and my school yearbook with messages from friends/teachers.*

Other things we might want to try could include: attending our medical appointments, taking our meds, being creative, spending time in nature, escaping with a book or film, undertaking any activities we find absorbing, pleasurable or distracting, decluttering, taking part in Blurt's #365daysofselfcare challenge.

## Final thoughts

### Start small

It can take a long time to form new habits – even when we're in good health. We musn't put too much pressure on ourselves. We might want to choose one healthy habit to introduce into our lives, and work

on it for a while before we introduce another. If we don't get off on the best foot, we must be kind to ourselves: a slow start is better than no start at all.

### Try different things

We may find that some healthy habits don't chime with us, they may feel uncomfortable, like they're not working – they might even upset us. If that's the case we need to give ourselves permission to let go and try something else. We're all different – so different things will work for each of us. Trial and error may need to apply.

### We deserve better

Although we are all unique, one thing that unites is the fact we don't deserve to feel the way we do. Depression is cruel and unfair. If there are things we can do that alleviate our symptoms – even for a moment – then we must allow ourselves to do them, no matter how loudly depression may protest. We deserve better.

*5 May 2017*

⇨ The above information is reprinted with kind permission from The Blurt Foundation. Please visit www.blurtitout.org for further information.

# Key facts

- Difficult events and experiences can leave us in low spirits or cause depression. (page 1)

- Life changes, such as getting a regular good night's sleep, keeping to a healthy diet, reducing your alcohol intake and getting regular exercise, can help you feel more in control and more able to cope. (page 1)

- According to the National Institute of Mental Health (NIMH) in the US, about 7% of the adult population suffer from major depression at any given time. (page 2)

- In the UK, figures show that 25% of people will experience a mental health problem each year and that a significant proportion of these problems are depression and anxiety related. (page 2)

- Around 10–15% of women are estimated to experience postnatal depression. (page 3)

- According to the NHS, about one person in every 100 in the UK is diagnosed with a bipolar disorder. (page 3)

- Health Survey for England found in 2014 that one in four people reported having been diagnosed with at least one mental illness at some point in their lives. A further 18% said they'd experienced an illness but hadn't been diagnosed. (page 4)

- Research by David Goldberg and Peter Huxley from 1980 found that one in four people in its sample had suffered some sort of mental disorder in a year. (page 5)

- Research shows that nearly one in five university students are affected with anxiety or depression. (page 6)

- Several other studies have found that mobile phone addiction, as well as excess smartphone use, is also associated with increased sleep disturbance, depression, anxiety and overall stress. (page 6)

- College students with a history of attention deficit hyperactivity disorder also have much higher rates of anxiety and depression. It is estimated that between two to eight per cent of college students struggle with symptoms of this disorder. (page 6)

- Research suggests that compared to men, women tend to ruminate (the technical term for 'over-thinking') more about stressors and have negative thoughts that cause depression. (page 8)

- Based on the 14-year-olds reporting of their emotional problems, 24 per cent of girls and nine per cent of boys suffer from depression. (page 10)

- One in four young people (24%) would not confide in someone if they were experiencing a mental health problem. (page 11)

- The vast majority of young people (78%) think there is a stigma attached to mental health issues. (page 11)

- Between 2008 and 2013, funding for the services dropped by 5.4 per cent in real terms so that in 2012/2013, only six per cent of the NHS' total mental health budget was spent on these services. (page 13)

- the number of young people attending A&E due to a psychiatric condition had doubled by 2014/2015, compared with 2010/2011. (page 13)

- Postnatal depression is more common than many realise. According to the charity Mind, around 10–15% of new mothers are affected. (page 14)

- Around seven to 20% of new mothers experience postnatal depression. (page 15)

- Four to five per cent of fathers experience significant depressive symptoms after their child is born. Some other studies claim that prevalence may be as high as ten per cent. (page 15)

- One in four adults will experience a mental illness at some point each year in the UK. Something we never hear is that we only expect to help 15 per cent of them. (page 16)

- Experts recommend that adults get between seven and nine hours of sleep a night. (page 18)

- Research tells us that if you sit still for more than 7 hours a day, you increase your likelihood of depression. (page 18)

- There's convincing evidence that 30 minutes of vigorous exercise three times a week is effective against depression, and anecdotal evidence that lighter exercise will have a beneficial effect, too. (page 19)

- Bipolar disorder can occur at any age, although it often develops between the ages of 15 and 19 and rarely develops after 40. (page 20)

- A survey of young people conducted by the London-based Royal Society for Public Health found that social media sites such as Instagram, which primarily focus on people's physical appearance, are "contributing to a generation of young people with body image and body confidence issues". (page 23)

- A 2015 study by the University of Missouri found that regularly using Facebook could lead to symptoms of depression if the site triggered feelings of envy in the user. (page 23)

- An estimated 350 million have depression worldwide. (page 30)

- Researchers analysed data from 522 trials involving 115,477 people and declared that the 21 most common antidepressants tested were effective at reducing the symptoms of depression. (page 32)

- Around one in 20 teenagers suffers from depression. (page 33)

# Glossary

## Antidepressants

These include tricyclic antidepressants (TCAs), selective serotonin re-uptake inhibitors (SSRIs) and monoamine oxidase inhibitors (MAOIs). Antidepressants work by boosting one or more chemicals (neurotransmitters) in the nervous system, which may be present in insufficient amounts during a depressive illness.

## Anxiety

Feeling nervous, worried or distressed, sometimes to a point where the person feels so overwhelmed that they find everyday life very difficult to handle.

## Bipolar disorder

Previously called manic depression, this illness is characterised by mood swings where periods of severe depression are balanced by periods of elation and over-activity (mania).

## Cognitive behavioural therapy (CBT)

A psychological treatment which assumes that behavioural and emotional reactions are learned over a long period. A cognitive therapist will seek to identify the source of emotional problems and develop techniques to overcome them.

## Counselling

Sometimes known as talk therapy, allows people to talk through their emotions and their decisions to hurt themselves. The counsellor or therapist provides support and may be able to teach self-harmer how to make more healthy choices in the future.

## Depression

Someone is said to be significantly depressed, or suffering from depression, when feelings of sadness or misery don't go away quickly and are so bad that they interfere with everyday life. Symptoms can also include low self-esteem and a lack of motivation. Depression can be triggered by a traumatic/difficult event (reactive depression), but not always (e.g. endogenous depression).

## Group therapy

These are meetings for people who are seeking help for a problem (in this case, self-harm or suicidal thoughts) and are led by trained specialists who provide professional advice and support.

## Light therapy

A treatment for seasonal affective disorder (SAD) which involves sitting near a light box for up to an hour a day.

## Medication

If a person is diagnosed with a mental illness such as clinical depression, medication may be prescribed (see Antidepressants). Some people might not want to take medication at all and prefer talking therapies, whilst others find a combination of both works best for them.

## Mental health

Sometimes called 'psychological well-being' or 'emotional health', mental health refers to the state of your mind and how a person can cope with everyday life. It is just as important as good physical health.

## Mindfulness

Mind-body based training that uses meditation, breathing and yoga techniques to help you focus on your thoughts and feelings. Mindfulness helps you manage your thoughts and feelings better, instead of being overwhelmed by them.

## Postnatal depression

Depression experienced by new mothers (but new fathers can experience it too). It is not known for certain what causes it, but some experts believe the sudden change in hormones after a baby's birth may be the trigger. Symptoms may include panic attacks, sleeping difficulties, overwhelming fear of death and feelings of inadequacy/being unable to cope.

## Seasonal affective disorder (SAD)

A type of depression which generally coincides with the approach of winter and is linked to shortening of daylight hours and lack of sunlight.

## Talking therapies

These involve talking and listening. Some therapists will aim to find the root cause of a sufferer's problem and help them deal with it, some will help to change behaviour and negative thoughts, while others simply offer support.

# Assignments

## Brainstorming

⇨ Brainstorm what you know about depression.

- What is depression?

- What is mindfullness?

- What are antidepressants?

- What is cognitive behavioural therapy?

- What does the term 'placebo' mean?

## Research

⇨ Do some research into the reasons people might become depressed. You should consider if it affects one gender more than the other? Does age come into things? Write a short report on your findings and share with the rest of your class.

⇨ In small groups, research the different types of help which are available to people suffering with depression. You could look at self-help groups, counselling and medication. Produce a graph to show your findings.

⇨ Research post-natal depression. Create a presentation explaining what post-natal depression is and the effect it can have not only on the sufferer but how it affects the people around them.

⇨ In pairs, research the way in which exercise can help people suffering from depression. Is any particular type of exercise best? How much exercise should a person do each week? Compile your data into a graph and present your findings to the class.

⇨ Do some research into how social media can affect a person's mood. Is this effect always negative? If not, what are the positive aspects for sufferers of depression? Make some notes on your findings and share with the rest of your class.

⇨ In small groups, do some research into bipolar disorder. How does this condition affect the sufferer? What can be done to help them in their everyday lives? Write a report on your findings and share with the rest of the class.

## Design

⇨ In small groups, design a leaflet that will highlight the issues of depression that teenagers today are facing. Your leaflet should offer help and advice on tackling these issues.

⇨ Produce a poster explaining what depression is and gives some information as to what help is available to sufferers.

⇨ Choose one of the articles from this book and create an illustration that highlights the key themes of the piece.

⇨ Design a poster which is to be displayed in colleges and universities encouraging students who might feel anxious or depressed, to seek help.

⇨ Read One in four girls is depressed at age 14, new study reveals, on page 10 and make an infographic from the information in the article.

## Oral

⇨ According to the article on page 6, "1 in five college students have anxiety or depression". In small groups discuss this statement.

⇨ Hold a class discussion on depression and low mood. What is the difference? Have you or your classmates suffered from either and how did it make them feel? Does your school discuss these issues with you? Do you think they should?

⇨ In pairs, go through this book and discuss the illustrations you come across. Think about what the artists were trying to portray with each illustration.

⇨ In pairs, list as many symptoms of depression as you can and the ways in which these might be alleviated. Give a short talk to the rest of your class on your findings.

⇨ In small groups, prepare a Prezi presentation that explains the signs and symptoms of depression. Share your presentation with your class.

## Reading/writing

⇨ Write a summary of the article Mindfulness is not a waste of time – it can help treat depression on page 37.

⇨ Imagine you are an Agony Aunt/Uncle writing for a national newspaper. A young girl has written to you admitting she is feeling very low and struggling with everyday tasks. Write a suitable reply giving advice and information on where she may look for support in order to tackle her issues.

⇨ Write a one-paragraph definition of 'depression'.

⇨ Write a one-paragraph definintion of 'mindfullness'.

⇨ Read the article on page 23 How bad is social media for your mental health and write a blog explaining the link between social media and isolation, depression and insomnia.

⇨ "Cuts to mental health services putting young people at risk, say experts" page 13. Write an essay exploring this statement. You should write at least 500 words.

⇨ Read What does depression feel like? Trust me – you really don't want to know on page 21 and write about your own experiences of depression.

# Acknowledgements

The publisher is grateful for permission to reproduce the material in this book. While every care has been taken to trace and acknowledge copyright, the publisher tenders its apology for any accidental infringement or where copyright has proved untraceable. The publisher would be pleased to come to a suitable arrangement in any such case with the rightful owner.

## Images

All images courtesy of iStock except pages 7, 14, 16, 22 and 39: Pixabay, pages 29, 33, 34, 38 and 39: Unsplash

## Illustrations

Don Hatcher: pages 25 & 36. Simon Kneebone: pages 8 & 19. Angelo Madrid: pages 3 & 31.

## Additional acknowledgements

With thanks to the Independence team: Shelley Baldry, Danielle Lobban, Jackie Staines and Jan Sunderland.

Tina Brand

Cambridge, June 2018